Social Issues in Literature

Violence in Suzanne Collins's *The Hunger Games* Trilogy

Other Books in the Social Issues in Literature Series:

Social Issues
in Literature

Violence in Suzanne Collins's *The Hunger Games* Trilogy

Gary Wiener, Book Editor

GREENHAVEN PRESS
A part of Gale, Cengage Learning

GALE
CENGAGE Learning

Farmington Hills, Mich • San Francisco • New York • Waterville, Maine
Meriden, Conn • Mason, Ohio • Chicago

GALE
CENGAGE Learning·

Elizabeth Des Chenes, *Director, Content Strategy*
Douglas Dentino, *Manager, New Product*

© 2015 Greenhaven Press, a part of Gale, Cengage Learning

WCN: 01-100-101

Gale and Greenhaven Press are registered trademarks used herein under license.

For more information, contact:
Greenhaven Press
27500 Drake Rd.
Farmington Hills, MI 48331-3535
Or you can visit our Internet site at gale.cengage.com

Articles in Greenhaven Press anthologies are often edited for length to meet page requirements. In addition, original titles of these works are changed to clearly present the main thesis and to explicitly indicate the author's opinion. Every effort is made to ensure that Greenhaven Press accurately reflects the original intent of the authors. Every effort has been made to trace the owners of copyrighted material.

Cover image © Byron Purvis/AdMedia/Corbis.

LIBRARY OF CONGRESS CATALOGING-IN-PUBLICATION DATA

Violence in Suzanne Collins's The Hunger Games Trilogy / edited by Gary Wiener.
    pages cm. -- (Social Issues in Literature)
    Summary: "This series brings together the disciplines of sociology and literature. It looks at a work of literature through the lens of the major social issue that is reflected in it"-- Provided by publisher.
    Includes bibliographical references and index.
    ISBN 978-0-7377-6990-6 (hardback) -- ISBN 978-0-7377-6991-3 (paperback)
    1. Collins, Suzanne--Criticism and interpretation. 2. Collins, Suzanne. Hunger Games. 3. Violence in literature. I. Wiener, Gary, editor.
    PS3603.O4558Z94 2015
    813'.6--dc23
                                                            2014010984

Printed in the United States of America
2 3 4 5 6   18 17 16 15 14

Contents

Chapter 1: Background on Suzanne Collins

Growing up as the daughter of a military man, Suzanne Collins learned of the nature of war at an early age. She used that knowledge to write the Underland Chronicles and *The Hunger Games* series.

Collins is known for fiercely guarding her privacy. Fortunately, she lives at a time when the media can do her publicity for her.

Just before the publication of *Mockingjay*, Suzanne Collins discusses important themes and symbols as well as biographical and literary influences of the trilogy.

The success of Collins's *The Hunger Games* trilogy has made her a celebrity, and she uses her platform as a writer to educate children about the reality of warfare.

Chapter 2: Violence in
The Hunger Games Trilogy

Introduction

Suzanne Collins has always had to confront violence. Her father was a career military man who fought in Vietnam, and Collins's first book after *The Hunger Games* trilogy, *Year of the Jungle*, is based on those biographical facts. Her first children's series, the Underland Chronicles, was full of carnage: As Collins herself notes, it contains "death, loss, and violence. The third book has biological warfare, the fourth book has genocide, the fifth book has a very graphic war. . . ."[1] And surely *The Hunger Games* series itself is notable first and foremost for its teen-on-teen combat. If all of that is not enough, in a bizarre twist of fate, the highly successful novelist lives in the community of Sandy Hook, Connecticut, where, in December 2012, a lone gunman, heavily armed like one of Collins's Careers, murdered twenty children and six teachers in a local elementary school.

Collins has endured much criticism for her violent plots. Writing for the *Huffington Post*, educator Tim King neatly coalesces much of the controversy:

> While the action kept me turning the page, I couldn't get past the fact that these are children who are not only dying, but doing the killing. Even Katniss isn't above the fray, as she kills four Tributes herself. In one particularly harrowing scene, one boy murders a twelve-year-old girl by trapping her in a net and thrusting a spear into her stomach; Katniss retaliates by killing the boy with an arrow to his neck. While not every death is played out this graphically, for me the idea that these kids are killing each other eclipses any other theme that might have been present.[2]

Explaining why she won't be taking her young child to see the cinematic version of the first book, *Time* magazine film critic Mary Pols states: "Nearly two dozen kids aged 12 to 18 die by machete, sword, blows with a brick, a spear to the chest, arrows, having their necks snapped. All damage inflicted by each other."[3]

Given such responses, it is not surprising that *The Hunger Games* and subsequent books in the series have appeared twice on the American Library Association's list of ten most challenged books, in large part due to their gruesome content.[4] However, as Irish young adult novelist Sarah Rees Brennan writes, readers are drawn to the repulsive nature of Collins's trilogy. The books tap into "the media's current fascination with manufactured reality, as well as humanity's enduring fascination with violence. The idea of children killing each other," she says, "is a horrible one to anyone, and yet so morbidly alluring."[5] Collins certainly did not invent gruesome storytelling or readers' attraction to such tales. After Sophocles's King Oedipus blinds himself in horrific fashion in *Oedipus Rex*, the playwright set down this response, which might characterize the mixed emotions with which readers react to Collins's most grotesque scenes: "I can't look, though there is much to see."[6]

Though violence is a staple of all eight young adult novels Collins has so far written, it was never her intention to celebrate bloodshed and brutality. Rather, Collins has stated numerous times that she wants to use her books to educate children about the reality of warfare. As Susan Hoover writes, "Suzanne was a member of a military family. Her grandfather served in World War I and her uncle in World War II. Even as a youngster she knew that her grandfather had been gassed and her uncle had survived shrapnel wounds."[7] Collins, the erstwhile military brat raised by a father who taught military history at West Point, knew from an early age the disruption that warfare brings to military families and the fear of wondering whether the family patriarch would ever return home. When asked what she wants readers to take away from her books, Collins is explicit about her view of warfare:

One of the reasons it's important for me to write about war is I really think that the concept of war, the specifics of war, the nature of war, the ethical ambiguities of war are introduced too late to children. I think they can hear them, understand them, know about them, at a much younger age without being scared to death by the stories. It's not comfortable for us to talk about, so we generally don't talk about these issues with our kids. But I feel that if the whole concept of war were introduced to kids at an earlier age, we would have better dialogues going on about it, and we would have a fuller understanding.[8]

When a reviewer opined that Collins's war stories were a metaphor for adolescence, Collins issued this correction: "I don't write about adolescence. I write about war. For adolescents."[9]

Collins believes that television, particularly reality television, desensitizes its audience to the nature of war and violence. In fact, the genesis of *The Hunger Games* stems from a night when Collins, channel surfing, flipped from a reality television show to news about the Iraq war. The images began to blur in her mind, and the idea for a televised reality battle show was born in part from her fear that modern audiences, particularly young viewers, could not distinguish what was real on television and what was not. As she told *Instructor* magazine:

The Hunger Games is a reality television program. An extreme one, but that's what it is. And while I think some of those shows can succeed on different levels, there's also the voyeuristic thrill, watching people being humiliated or brought to tears or suffering physically. And that's what I find very disturbing. There's this potential for desensitizing the audience so that when they see real tragedy playing out on the news, it doesn't have the impact it should. It all just blurs into one program. And I think it's very important not just for young people, but for adults to make sure they're making the distinction. Because the young soldiers dying in the war in Iraq, it's not going to end at the commercial break. It's not something fabricated, it's not a game. It's your life.[10]

In depicting the brutality of warfare in the Underland Chronicles and *The Hunger Games* trilogy, Collins does not treat her loyal readers gently. In both series, important, even beloved, characters are fated to die. Perhaps J.K. Rowling set the standard for such tragedy in contemporary young adult literature. Midway through writing her Harry Potter series, she warned her readers that there would be deaths and that they would be horrible to write. In fact, Rowling even considered killing her protagonist, or, at least, says she did: "That was a—it was felt to be a possibility that the hero would die," she told NBC's Meredith Vieira. "And that's what I was aiming for, that you really felt that anyone was up for grabs."[11] Before the series concluded, Rowling kept her promise and the deaths of certain popular characters left readers' mouths agape. "Fred [Weasley], Lupin and Tonks really caused me a lot of pain," she said.[12] In the Underland Chronicles, Collins follows suit, though her victims are most often nonhuman. Even so, the demise of Gregor's beloved bat and bondmate, Ares, comes as something of a shock. However, readers are pretty much assured throughout that Gregor's toddler sister and sidekick, Boots, will survive the series, even though she is placed in numerous near-catastrophic situations from which no real two-year-old could possibly emerge unscathed.

It is in *The Hunger Games* series where Collins's willingness to kill off her characters tops Rowling and even her former self. As reviewer Katie Roiphe suggests, "Like the evil Capitol that controls and shadows its world, the trilogy tends to use the things we are attached to against us."[13] We get a sense of just how morbid the series is likely to be when Katniss's first true ally, Rue, is murdered in grisly fashion. However, Rue's slaying foreshadows a far more important death that is to follow in the final book, *Mockingjay*. Primrose

Everdeen's death in the novel's last pages comes as such a shock that when Collins's editor, Rosemary Stimola, read it in draft form, she advised Collins, "No, don't do it."[14] Collins was adamant, however. "Oh, but it has to be," Collins told Stimola. "This is not a fairy tale; it's a war, and in war, there are tragic losses that must be mourned."[15] The implications of this horrifying death are profound. It was Katniss's protectiveness of Prim and her need to prevent her younger sister from becoming a victim of the Hunger Games after Effie Trinket drew Prim's name at the reaping that drove Katniss to take her place. From this one plot point, the entire trilogy—Katniss's identification as the Mockingjay, the ensuing district-by-district rebellion, and the Mockingjay war itself—stems. In this context, the irony of Prim's death is pervasive. All of Katniss's victories—her quest, her triumph over Snow and the Capitol, and the independence of the districts—are rendered Pyrrhic in light of Prim's demise. No fairy tale, indeed.

Then again, if Collins's declaration that she always conceived of *The Hunger Games* as a trilogy is to be believed, it is possible that she knew of Prim's fate, and foreshadowed it, from the first moments of the first book. *The Hunger Games* opens with these words: "When I wake up, the other side of the bed is cold. My fingers stretch out, seeking Prim's warmth but finding only the rough canvas cover of the mattress."[16] Prim's death torments her older sister for years after the Mockingjay war ends. At the conclusion of the third book, two of Katniss's observations echo the trilogy's opening line with the new understanding of what war has cost her: "I wake screaming from nightmares of mutts and lost children."[17] Only two pages later, in the epilogue, Katniss refers to what she will tell her own children about her brutal past: "I'll tell them that on bad mornings, it feels impossible to take pleasure in anything because I'm afraid it could be taken away."[18] In a series where the central premise involves twenty-three children dying so that one may live, perhaps no death should be entirely surprising. Rather, in Rowling's words, readers must acknowledge that "anyone [is] up for grabs."

Prim is not the only victim of the Mockingjay rebellion. Fan favorite Cinna is hauled off by the authorities after designing Katniss's subversive wedding dress:

> Suddenly the door behind him bursts open and three Peace-keepers spring into the room. Two pin Cinna's arms behind him and cuff him while the third hits him in the temple with such force he's knocked to his knees. But they keep hitting him with metal-studded gloves, opening gashes on his face and body. I'm screaming my head off, banging on the unyielding glass, trying to reach him. The Peacekeepers ignore me completely as they drag Cinna's limp body from the room. All that's left are the smears of blood on the floor.[19]

Katniss barely has time to consider what has happened to her devoted stylist before she is thrust into the fray of the Quarter Quell. She never sees Cinna again. Similarly, *Catching Fire* hero and heartthrob, Finnick Odair, is knocked off almost as an afterthought: "Far below, I can just make out Finnick, struggling to hang on as three mutts tear at him . . . one yanks back his head to take the death bite. . . . Then it's over."[20] It is an unexpected, unheroic end for the cocky, blindingly handsome former Hunger Games champion.

To those who accuse Collins of excessive violence, particularly in books aimed at young adults, Collins's supporters counter that today's young people have grown accustomed to a violent world and that the trilogy's depiction of brutality always has a larger purpose. When Collins was a young girl, her father would take the family to famous battlefields. Of those educational excursions, Collins would later say, "It wasn't enough to visit a battlefield, we needed to know why the battle occurred, how it played out, and the consequences. Fortunately, he had a gift for presenting history as a fascinating story. He had a good sense of exactly how much a child could handle, which is quite a bit."[21] Following in the family tradition, Collins takes her readers to her own, albeit imaginary, battlefields, so that they, too, may learn from the combat of others. Further, she believes that her young readers can handle "quite a bit."

The viewpoints that follow consider the violence in Collins's trilogy from a wide range of perspectives. The writers are former soldiers, professors, pacifists, religious leaders, and bloggers. Despite their differing insights, almost all agree that the bloodbath depicted in *The Hunger Games* trilogy does have a greater purpose, and that while the Capitol may promote senseless violence, Collins does not.

Notes

1. "Suzanne Collins," *Newsmakers*. Vol. 2. Detroit, MI: Gale, 2011. *Gale Biography in Context*.

2. Tim King, "Hungry for More: The Hunger Games Misses the Mark on Teen Violence," *Huffington Post*, March 23, 2012. http://www.huffingtonpost.com /tim-king/hungry-for-more-the-hunge_b_ 1374055.html.

3. Mary Pols, "Why I'm NOT Taking My 8-Year-Old to *The Hunger Games*," *Time*, March 22, 2012. http://ideas.time.com/2012/03/22/why-im-not-taking-my-8 -year-old-to-the-hunger-games/#ixzz2kv5SXW9o.

4. "Frequently Challenged Books of the 21st Century," American Library Association. http://www.ala.org/bbooks/frequentlychallengedbooks/top10.

5. Sarah Rees Brennan, "Why So Hungry for the Hunger Games?," in *The Girl Who Was on Fire: Your Favorite Authors on Suzanne Collins' Hunger Games Trilogy*. Ed. Leah Wilson. Dallas, TX: BenBella, 2010.

6. Sophocles, *Oedipus Rex*. p. 3.

7. Elizabeth Hoover, *Suzanne Collins*. Detroit, MI: Lucent Books, 2012, p. 13.

8. Rick Margolis, "The Last Battle: With 'Mockingjay' on Its Way, Suzanne Collins Weighs In on Katniss and the Capitol," *School Library Journal*, August 2010.

9. Susan Dominus, "Suzanne Collins' War Stories for Kids," *New York Times*, April 8, 2011. http://www.nytimes.com/2011/04/10/magazine/mag-10collins-t.html ?pagewanted=all&_r=0.

10. Suzanne Collins, "Sit Down with Suzanne Collins: The Author of *The Hunger Games* Says We Need to Get Real About War, Violence, and TV," *Instructor* [1990] September–October 2010.

11. "Interview with J.K. Rowling," *Dateline*, NBC, July 29, 2007.

12. "Spoiler Alert! Rowling Discusses Harry's Fate Here," *USA Today*, July 25, 2007.

13. Katie Roiphe, "Survivor," *New York Times Book Review*, September 12, 2010.

14. Susan Dominus, "Suzanne Collins' War Stories for Kids," *New York Times*, April 8, 2011. http://www.nytimes.com/2011/04/10/magazine/mag-10collins-t.html ?pagewanted=all&_r=0.

15. Ibid.

16. Suzanne Collins, *The Hunger Games*. New York: Scholastic, 2010, p. 3.

17. Suzanne Collins, *Mockingjay*. New York: Scholastic, 2010, p. 388.

18. Ibid., p. 390.

19. Suzanne Collins, *Catching Fire*. New York: Scholastic, 2010, pp. 262–3.

20. Suzanne Collins, *Mockingjay*. New York: Scholastic, 2010, pp. 312–3.

21. Suzanne Collins, "A Conversation: Questions and Answers," Scholastic. http:// www.scholastic.com/thehungergames/about-the-author.htm.

Chronology

1962

Suzanne Collins is born on August 10, 1962, in Hartford, Connecticut, to Michael and Jane Collins.

1968

The family moves to Indiana. Michael Collins serves in the Vietnam War.

1973

The family moves to Brussels, Belgium.

1980

Collins graduates from the Alabama School of Fine Arts and enrolls in Indiana University.

1985

Collins graduates from Indiana University with a double major in theater and telecommunications.

1987

Collins moves to New York City and studies screenwriting at New York University (NYU).

1989

Collins earns a master of fine arts (MFA) degree from NYU's Tisch School of the Arts.

1991

Collins begins writing for children's television. She coauthors the teleplay *Santa, Baby!*

1993

Collins writes two episodes for the Nickelodeon show *Clarissa Explains It All.*

1994
Collins's son, Charlie, is born.

1997–8
Collins writes for the Nickelodeon show *The Mystery Files of Shelby Woo.*

1999
Collins's daughter, Isabel, is born.

2000–1
Collins co-creates and writes for the television show *Generation O!*

2003
The family moves to Connecticut. Collins publishes *Gregor the Overlander*, the first of five books in the Underland Chronicles.

Collins serves as head writer for Scholastic's television show *Clifford's Puppy Days.*

2004
Collins publishes *Gregor and the Prophecy of Bane.*

2005
Collins publishes *Gregor and the Curse of the Warmbloods* and the children's picture book *When Charlie McButton Lost Power.*

2006
Collins publishes *Gregor and the Marks of Secret.*

2007
Collins publishes *Gregor and the Code of Claw*, the final book in the Underland Chronicles.

2008
Collins publishes *The Hunger Games*, the first book of her young adult trilogy. Collins writes for the children's television show *Wow! Wow! Wubbzy!*

2009

Collins publishes *Catching Fire*, the second book in *The Hunger Games* trilogy.

2010

Collins publishes *Mockingjay*, the final book in *The Hunger Games* trilogy. Collins is named one of *Time* magazine's one hundred most influential people.

2011

Collins cowrites the screenplay for the movie *Ticket Out*, starring Ray Liotta.

2012

The film adaptation of *The Hunger Games*, the first movie in a series of four based on Collins's trilogy, is released.

2013

Collins publishes the autobiographical picture book *Year of the Jungle*. The film adaptation of *Catching Fire* is released. Filming for *Mockingjay* begins.

CHAPTER 1

Background on
Suzanne Collins

The Life of Suzanne Collins

Authors and Artists for Young Adults

Authors and Artists for Young Adults includes fascinating and entertaining facts about writers, artists, film directors, graphic novelists, and other creative personalities. International in scope, each volume contains twenty to twenty-five entries, offering personal behind-the-scenes information, portraits, movie stills, bibliographies, a cumulative index, and more.

Growing up as the daughter of a career military man who served in Vietnam, Suzanne Collins understood the nature of war and violence from a young age. While many parents want to shelter their children from these subjects, Collins has made war an integral part of the Underland Chronicles and The Hunger Games *trilogy. Both collections have garnered positive reviews from critics. The Hunger Games series has been lauded for its ruthless depictions of violence and its compelling storytelling. Collins is particularly proud that her books engage even reluctant readers who might not otherwise pick up a book.*

Suzanne Collins finds inspiration for her award-winning, best-selling novels from a variety of sources—Greek mythology, classic literature, television, and her own life. Collins's works present exotic new worlds that feel real, and they address timeless issues that are never sugarcoated. Her endearing characters and complex plot twists hook readers and make them long for her next book. In her novels, Collins demonstrates "the light touch of a writer who truly understands writing for young people," Gabrielle Zevin commented in the *New York Times Book Review*.

"Suzanne Collins," *Authors and Artists for Young Adults*, vol. 86, Gale, 2011. Copyright © 2006 Cengage Learning.

Though her critically acclaimed series, the Underland Chronicles and *The Hunger Games* trilogy, could be considered sci-fi or fantasy, to Collins, "they're absolutely, first and foremost, war stories," as she remarked to *School Library Journal* interviewer Rick Margolis. Since adults tend to shelter children from violence, many writers shy away from it in books aimed at young readers. Collins, however, prefers to tackle those issues head-on. "One of the reasons it's important for me to write about war," she told Margolis, "is I really think that the concept of war, the specifics of war, the nature of war, the ethical ambiguities of war are introduced too late to children." She continued, "It's not comfortable for us to talk about, so we generally don't talk about these issues with our kids. But I feel that if the whole concept of war were introduced to kids at an earlier age, we would have better dialogues going on about it, and we would have a fuller understanding."

Growing Up Unshielded

The author's beliefs about discussing violence and conflict with children are derived from her personal experience. Her father was career U.S. Air Force, serving in Vietnam when she was six. "If your parent is deployed and you are that young, you spend the whole time wondering where they are and waiting for them to come home," she told *New York Times* interviewer Susan Dominus. "As time passes and the absence is longer and longer, you become more and more concerned— but you don't really have the words to express your concern. There's only this continued absence." Collins—the youngest of four—remembers watching news footage of the war on TV; although the images were frightening, Collins's parents helped alleviate some of her concerns by communicating openly about the context of war. Her father, who also taught at West Point, "felt that it was part of his responsibility to teach us, his children, about history and war," she related to Margolis. "When I think back, at the center of all this is the question of

Best-selling author Suzanne Collins said that the best feeling of being a writer for her is the idea that she might have contributed to a child's enjoyment of reading. © Michael Hurcomb/Corbis.

what makes a necessary war—at what point is it justifiable or unavoidable?" The author further noted that her father "would discuss these things at a level that he thought we could understand and were acceptable for our age. But, really, he thought a lot was acceptable for our age, and I approach my books in the same way."

As a youngster, Collins was exposed to a variety of literature. In fifth and sixth grades, her English teacher, Mrs. Vance, would read tales by [American author] Edgar Allan Poe to her students on rainy days. Collins recalled in an *Instructor* interview "sitting around just wide-eyed" and "riveted" by stories such as "The Tell-Tale Heart" and "The Mask of the Red Death." As a teenager, her favorite books reflected her passion for exploring social issues. *Anna Karenina* by [Russian novelist] Leo Tolstoy and *The Heart Is a Lonely Hunter* by [American novelist] Carson McCullers describe the effects of hardship and severe circumstances on people, *Nineteen Eighty-Four* by [British author] George Orwell was an example of how human nature begets oppression, and *Lord of the Flies* by [British novelist] William Golding introduced generations of young readers to child-on-child violence. All of these books influenced, and possibly sparked, the stories that Collins would grow up to tell.

Collins's career in writing for a young audience began in television. She penned screenplays for several Nickelodeon shows, such as *The Mystery Files of Shelby Woo* and the Emmy-nominated *Clarissa Explains It All*. She cowrote the Rankin/Bass Christmas special *Santa, Baby!* and was the head writer on Scholastic Entertainment's *Clifford's Puppy Days*. While working on the Kids WB show *Generation O!*, she met author James Proimos, who suggested that she try her hand at writing children's books. "I find there isn't a great deal of difference technically in how you approach a story, no matter what age it's for," she remarked to a *Scholastic* interviewer. "I started out as a playwright for adult audiences. When television work came along, it was primarily for children. But whatever age you're writing for, the same rules of plot, character, and theme apply. You just set up a world and try to remain true to it."

Not Wonderland, but Underland

While pondering Lewis Carroll's *Alice in Wonderland*, Collins was struck by the notion that contemporary readers, many of whom were raised in urban environments, may not relate to the book's pastoral [country] setting. Allowing her imagination to soar, she created what a *Kirkus Reviews* critic described as "a strange underground land of giant cockroaches, rideable bats, and violet-eyed humans," which became the setting for *Gregor the Overlander*, the first book in her middle grade sci-fi series the Underland Chronicles. As Collins told Jen Rees in an interview on her home page, she selected the Underland setting because "I liked the fact that this world was teeming under New York City and nobody was aware of it. That you could be going along preoccupied with your own problems and then whoosh! You take a wrong turn in your laundry room and suddenly a giant cockroach is right in your face. No magic, no space or time travel, there's just a ticket to another world behind your clothes dryer."

In the novel, Collins introduces readers to her series' protagonists, eleven-year-old Gregor and his baby sister, Boots. After the pair tumble down an air duct in their apartment building, they find themselves in Underland, a strange otherworld whose inhabitants believe Gregor is the Overland Warrior, the person foretold in prophecy who would liberate them from a warlike race of gigantic rats. Kitty Flynn wrote in *Horn Book*, "Collins evokes this dark, cavernous world and its archaic, agrarian society with a sure hand and sends a reluctant Gregor on the classic hero's journey." Similarly, a *Publishers Weekly* critic noted that the author "does a grand job of worldbuilding, with a fine economy of words—no unnecessary details bog down either the setting or the invigorating story."

Gregor and the Prophecy of Bane, the second book in the series, depicts the further adventures of the brave youngster. After Boots is kidnapped and taken back to Underland, Gregor tracks her to the city of Regalia. There he learns of the prophecy of Bane, which decrees that he must battle an enormous white rat, and Gregor's quest for his adversary takes him on a perilous journey across a subterranean sea. Beth L. Meister of *School Library Journal* wrote that "the hazards and beauties of the subterranean Underland are fully realized and clearly presented." Flynn offered praise for the sequel, noting that the work "features Collins's careful attention to detail, pacing, and character development."

In the third book, *Gregor and the Curse of the Warmbloods*, "Collins maintains the momentum, charm, and vivid settings of the original title," according to Tasha Saecker in *School Library Journal*. Accompanied by Boots, a rat named Ripred, and a cockroach named Temp, Gregor must find a cure for a plague that threatens the lives of all the mammals in Underland, including his mother, who has ventured to the strange world, and his friend Ares, a giant bat. "This offering takes on an even darker tone than the earlier ones," a contributor in *Kirkus Reviews* observed, and Flynn, while stating that "Collins seems to have hit her stride with this page-turner," likewise noted the novel's "shocking and sobering conclusion," which sees Gregor and Boots leaving their mother in Underland when they return home.

Collins explores the socio-philosophical impact of war itself in the final two books of the series, *Gregor and the Marks of Secret* and *Gregor and the Code of Claw*. In the former, Gregor discovers evidence of a genocide while investigating a distress call from the mice of Underland, and in the final installment in the series, the protagonist learns of a prophecy foretelling his own death. The climax of the story approaches as Gregor prepares his warriors for a great battle with the giant rats, led by the despotic Bane, in the underground city of Regalia. A contributor in *Kirkus Reviews* stated, "Perhaps Collins's greatest achievement in these tales is the effortless introduction of weighty geopolitical ethics into rip-roaring adventure." Flynn applauded the concluding volume in the series, commenting that the author "delivers more of what's made this series so compelling: vivid action scenes, detailed military machinations, and nuanced character development."

A Futuristic Theseus

For her best-selling *The Hunger Games* trilogy, Collins pulled from classical roots, specifically the Greek myth about Theseus of Athens, who slew the Minotaur and ended the tyrannical reign of King Minos of Crete. After defeating Athens, King Minos wanted to ensure that the Athenians were kept oppressed and subjugated. So every nine years, he forced fourteen of their children to enter an elaborate labyrinth in Crete, where they would be devoured by the Minotaur, a half-man, half-bull monster who lived in it. "Even as a kid, I could appreciate how ruthless this was," the author commented in a *Scholastic* interview. "Crete was sending a very clear message: 'Mess with us and we'll do something worse than kill you. We'll kill your children.' And the thing is, it was allowed; the parents sat by powerless to stop it."

Collins also found inspiration from the story of Spartacus, a slave turned gladiator who, forced to fight to the death for the entertainment of the citizens in ancient Rome, led a rebellion against his oppressors. The author also drew from a contemporary source—television—for her trilogy. She related the moment the idea for the series came to her in an interview with James Blasingame in the *Journal of Adolescent & Adult Literacy*: "I was very tired and I was lying in bed channel surfing. I happened upon a reality program, recorded live, that pitted young people against each other for money. As I sleepily watched, the lines of reality started to blur for me, and the idea for the book emerged."

Like both Theseus and Spartacus, *The Hunger Games* heroine Katniss Everdeen is thrust into a life-or-death contest mandated by a ruthless government. The trilogy's events take place in a dystopian future. The United States is no more; in its place is Panem, which is comprised of twelve districts and a Capitol city. More than seventy years ago, there had been thirteen districts, but an uprising by the citizens against the Capitol was crushed and District Thirteen was demolished. In addition to ongoing, dictatorial control by the Capitol—including electrified security fences around the districts and the presence of permanent peacekeeping forces within them—the government came up with another way to discourage future revolts: Each year, the districts must supply two tributes—a boy and a girl—to take part in the Hunger Games. Participants are chosen by lottery, and they are forced to battle each other in an outdoor arena. The televised spectacle continues until a lone survivor remains. Winners reap huge financial rewards for themselves and their districts, and they are exempt from future competitions, although they must serve as mentors for the subsequent tributes from their district. District Twelve has had only two winners in the history of the games, and the only living victor is a drunk named Haymitch.

The Hunger Games

In the first book of the series, *The Hunger Games*, readers meet Katniss, a sixteen-year-old girl from impoverished District Twelve. In the five years since her father died in a mine explosion, Katniss has helped support her mother and little sister, Prim, by illegally hunting beyond the district's fences. This year is the first that Prim is eligible to be selected as a Hunger Games participant. The odds of a twelve-year-old being chosen are slim, because entries are cumulative. In addition, eligible participants can trade additional lottery entries for food supplies—and many poor teenagers do so to help feed their families. For instance, Katniss's best friend, Gale, an eighteen-year-old boy who harbors romantic feelings for her, has forty-two entries in the drawing; Katniss herself has twenty. The entire town is shocked, therefore, when Prim's name is chosen. Katniss volunteers to take her sister's place and joins the male selection, Peeta Mellark, son of the local baker. Katniss is not friends with Peeta, but remembers a favor he did for her in the devastating months after her father's death. This starts a complicated relationship: She feels indebted to him, but she does not want to become friends with someone she may have to kill.

The two stunned teenagers are taken to the Capitol, given makeovers, and paraded in front of the enthusiastic crowds, which take a liking to both of them. The opulence of the Capitol is amazing to the duo, as is the amount and quality of food available. Too soon, though, they are transported to the arena, where the life-or-death struggle begins. Katniss's hunting skills serve her well. As other tributes are killed and their bodies removed, Katniss more fully comprehends the situation into which she has been forced. She does care about some of the other contestants and her resentment and anger toward the Capitol builds. She stubbornly refuses to be merely a pawn in the government's game, and when she and Peeta end up as the last remaining contestant, she comes up with a plan to simultaneously avoid a gut-wrenching decision and to force the Capitol's hand regarding the official ending of the games. Collins does not hold back in her vivid depictions of the contest's more gruesome aspects, yet the violence is not gratuitous. "Rather than being repellent, the violence is strangely hypnotic," *Time* reviewer Lev Grossman wrote. "It's fairy-tale violence, Brothers Grimm [German folklorists] violence—not a cheap thrill but a symbol of something deeper."

The Hunger Games garnered strong reviews. *Horn Book* contributor Jonathan Hunt called the work "a compulsively readable blend of science fiction, survival story, unlikely romance, and social commentary," and *School Library Journal* critic Jane Henriksen Baird remarked that "the plot is tense, dramatic, and engrossing." In the words of Stephen King, writing in *Entertainment Weekly*, "Collins is an efficient no-nonsense prose stylist with a pleasantly dry sense of humor. Reading *The Hunger Games* is as addictive (and as violently simple) as playing one of those shoot-it-if-it-moves video games in the lobby of the local eightplex; you know it's not real, but you keep plugging in quarters anyway."

Catching Fire

The second book of the series, *Catching Fire*, picks up six months after the Hunger Games' conclusion. Katniss's life is altered: her family is well-off, but she has changed, as has her relationship with Gale, who is jealous that Katniss faked a romance with Peeta as a strategy in the games. Peeta and Katniss are both plagued by nightmares, and Peeta was hurt to find that Katniss's feelings for him were not real. The two are forced together again, to take part in the Hunger Games victory tour, which makes stops in every district. Prior to the tour launch, President Snow makes an unexpected visit to Katniss's home. Her stunt at the end of the games means she is now his enemy, and he threatens both Katniss and her family if she does anything to foment a rebellion. He also insists that she convincingly depict being in love with Peeta. Despite her assurances, Katniss unintentionally prompts an antigovernment display in one of the districts.

There is no immediate reprisal from the President, and Katniss assumes her next official duty will be to serve as a mentor to District Twelve's tributes in this year's Hunger Games. It's the seventy-fifth anniversary of the games, and the contests held at twenty-five-year intervals are called Quarter Quells and have additional and unexpected features. This time, the Capitol changes the rules and announces that participants will be chosen from each district's roster of past winners. District Twelve has only three living victors. Katniss is forced back into the action, as is Peeta, who volunteers to take Haymitch's place when he is chosen. President Snow didn't foresee the negative reaction to this change by the usually pliable residents of the Capitol. They aren't happy, because the victors are well-loved celebrities and they don't want them to die. In the lead-up to the games, all of the contestants gather in the Capitol and are given opportunities to get to know each other. When the live interview sessions take place, Peeta has another bombshell for the audience that once again makes Katniss the contestant to protect. But they all underestimate President Snow's determination to hold absolute power over the country. In addition to facing experienced killers in the games, the arena itself acts as an enemy, holding deadly dangers. A portion of the contestants conspire to keep Peeta and Katniss alive and to destroy the arena. When the destruction begins, rebels appear to rescue the participants: They get Katniss, but Peeta is captured by the government. Katniss's family is safe, as is Gale, but District Twelve is razed in retribution.

Unlike so many trilogies where the second book lags, Zevin wrote in the *New York Times Book Review,* "Collins has done that rare thing. She has written a sequel that improves upon the first book." According to Hunt, "Collins has once again delivered a page-turning blend of plot and character with an inventive setting and provocative themes." A contributor to *Publishers Weekly* complimented the author's portrayal of Katniss, whose "bravery, honesty and wry cynicism carry the narrative," while Zevin felt that the protagonist "is more sophisticated in this book, and her observations are more acute." *Booklist's* Ian Chipman credited Collins for her "crystalline, unadorned prose" and remarked, "Honestly, this book only needs to be good enough to satisfy its legions of fans. Fortunately, it's great."

Mockingjay

The final book in the trilogy, *Mockingjay,* opens with Katniss recovering from her physical injuries from the Hunger Games but engulfed in emotional pain. The destruction of District Twelve is eating away at her; ninety percent of the population perished in the government's attack, and she feels responsible for all of the deaths. The survivors have taken refuge in District Thirteen, where the rebel leaders are headquartered. War rages between the districts and the Capitol, and Katniss is pressured to serve as the symbolic leader of the rebels, the Mockingjay. She initially resists, but when she discovers Peeta is alive and likely being tortured, she agrees to join the rebels. They launch a successful mission to rescue Peeta, but find him dangerous and nearly unrecognizable, as a result of brainwashing by the government.

Katniss joins the other soldiers to train for an assault on the Capitol. Her friend Gale also takes part, but differs from Katniss because he is a true believer in the rebellion. He is also smart enough to think up unique strategies and ruthless enough to carry them out. When the rebels reach the Capitol, the government uses not only its force but also all of the tricks from past Hunger Games against them. The Capitol falls, but Katniss is severely wounded in an explosion that kills one of her family members. The closing chapters describe the transition of governmental leadership, which Katniss influences, and her return home, where she tries to put her life back together and work through the trauma of her experiences.

Mockingjay, is a "compelling, powerful, intense novel," according to Deborah L. Dubois in *Voice of Youth Advocates.* "Collins is absolutely ruthless in her depictions of war in all its cruelty, violence, and loss," observed Baird, and Hunt believed that the author "has brought the most compelling science-fiction saga of the past several years to a satisfying and provocative conclusion." "The trilogy balances seriousness with special effects, a fundamental furious darkness with fast-paced storytelling, so that the books manage to be simultaneously disturbing and fun," wrote Katie Roiphe in the *New York Times Book Review.* "They contain a sharp satire of celebrity culture, mindless tabloidism and decadence, as well as crusading teenagers trying to save the world; but they also resist our hunger for clear definitions of good and evil, our sentimental need for a worthwhile cause, our desire for happy or simple endings, or even for the characters we like not to be killed or tortured or battered or bruised in graphic ways."

Truthful Yet Entertaining Stories

Collins does not shield her young readers from the violence of war, nor does she sugarcoat the moral implications and ambiguities. She presents truthful yet thoroughly entertaining stories that keep readers thinking and grappling with issues long after the books are closed. "One of the most memorable things I hear is when someone tells me that my books got a reluctant reader to read," she noted in her *Instructor* conversation. "They'll say, 'You know, there's this kid and he wouldn't touch a book and his parents found him under a blanket with a flashlight after bedtime because he couldn't wait to find out what happened in the next chapter.' That's just the best feeling. The idea that you might have contributed to a child's enjoyment of reading."

Suzanne Collins Is Something of a Mystery

Claire Armistead

Claire Armistead is the literary editor for the Guardian, *a British daily newspaper. She has worked as a theater critic for the* Hampstead & Highgate Express, *the* Financial Times, *and the* Guardian. *Armistead has contributed essays to* New Performance *and* Women: A Cultural Review. *She makes regular appearances on radio and television as a cultural commentator on literature and the arts.*

There are very few authors who can break into the universal cultural consciousness, Armistead writes, but Suzanne Collins seems to have joined the ranks of the J.K. Rowlings and Roald Dahls. However, the woman behind the novels is not well known. Collins has zealously guarded her privacy, which is in striking contrast to the plot of The Hunger Games, *where characters act out their lives and deaths in front of television cameras. Collins's greatest triumph in the novels lies in the character of Katniss, who is extremely well delineated by the author. She appeals to readers of both sexes, which is highly unusual. Despite Collins's reluctance to use the media herself, she has the good fortune to live at a time when the media can provide all the publicity* The Hunger Games *needs without her help.*

There are many best-selling children's authors but only rarely do any come along who break through into the universal cultural consciousness. [British author] C.S. Lewis did it, as did [British authors] Roald Dahl and J.K. Rowling. Now along comes Suzanne Collins, a 49-year-old from Connecticut, in the US, with *The Hunger Games* trilogy.

Claire Armistead, "Suzanne Collins: Hunger Games Author Who Found Rich Pickings in Dystopia," *The Guardian*, April 27, 2012. Copyright Guardian News & Media Ltd 2012.

A Bit of a Mystery

It's too early to know how durable this series will prove, but the signs so far are good. It has spent more than 100 weeks on the *New York Times* best-seller list. The film has made converts of even the most curmudgeonly critics, grossing more than $531m[illion] worldwide in its first four weeks. More than 1m[illion] copies of the books are now in print in the UK [United Kingdom], and last month [in March 2012] Amazon announced that Collins had become the best-selling Kindle author so far.

The woman behind the phenomenon is a bit of a mystery. Collins wrote for children's TV before turning to novels. She co-wrote the screenplay of *The Hunger Games* and is married to a TV actor—so knows a bit about the media circus—but she doesn't do publicity, hasn't even met her UK publishers, and seemed to tread the red carpet reluctantly at the film's Los Angeles premiere.

On her website, she is photographed in Central Park in New York, nose to snout with a toy rat, her long hair flowing witchily around her. "If you've read my fantasy series, the Underland Chronicles, you will have a clue as to why I chose this photo," she writes, offering no help to any visiting *Hunger Games* fan who had imagined her refulgent in a flaming robe.

Indeed, the whole site seems oddly out of synch. [Editor's note: It has since been updated]. Her biography page and sole author interview are all about the Underland Chronicles, a five-part fantasy series starring an 11-year-old boy, which preceded *The Hunger Games*. Apart from a scattering of jacket pictures and excitable press quotes, the only mention of the books that have made her name is: "Her next series, *The Hunger Games* trilogy, is an international bestseller."

The Hunger Games and the Media

Is her reluctance to self-publicise innocent or knowing? Either way, it's striking in the context of *The Hunger Games*, which is

Author Suzanne Collins poses for a portrait session on the rooftop of the Scholastic offices in New York City in 2009. © Todd Plitt/Contour/ Getty Images.

set in a nation, Panem, in which everything is televised. A fragmented post-apocalyptic society is ruled by the fascistic Capitol, which keeps the masses quiet by feeding them reality war games featuring teenagers who must fight to the last one standing.

The players who are "reaped" to play in the games are battling on two fronts: their primitive hand-to-hand combat, with whatever weapons come to hand, is mirrored by a more devious play for the sympathy—and sponsorship—of the people who are forced to watch. So the central character, Katniss, is both a warrior and a reality TV star with her own personal stylist. In these Hunger Games, it's not enough to be deadly with a bow and arrow; to survive, Katniss must seduce viewers into sending her food and medicine.

In a video interview made for her publisher, Scholastic, Collins says that the idea came to her when she was channel surfing one night in bed. "I was very tired . . . and I was flipping through images on reality television where these young people were competing for a million dollars or whatever, then I was seeing footage from the Iraq war, and these two things began to fuse together in a very unsettling way, and that is the moment where I got the idea for Katniss's story."

War and the Media

But the troubling relationship between war and the media was impressed on her long before that night. Her father spent his career in the US Air Force and served in Vietnam. "My mother tried really hard to protect us but occasionally after afternoon cartoons of whatever was on . . . the nightly news would come on and I'd see footage from the war zone and I would hear the word Vietnam and I would know my dad was over there and it was a very frightening experience for me."

The globe-trotting life of an Air Force family inspired two other preoccupations that would become central to the trilogy—it gave her space to develop a fascination with classical mythology, and it took her to lots of battlefields, ancient and modern, which her historically minded father would explain to his four children in strategic detail. The idea of a vengeful state that sends young people to be slaughtered came from Theseus and the Minotaur, while the games themselves are modelled on the gladiatorial contests of ancient Rome.

Katniss Everdeen as Hero

At the heart of the books is the character of Katniss—an action heroine, whose ambivalence about herself and others does not merely decorate the story but drives the plot.

It's a trick that is particularly admired by the novelist and screenwriter Anthony Horowitz, whose Alex Rider books have been one of the most successful action series in the UK over the past decade. He says: "Suzanne Collins has pulled off a remarkable coup, producing a female character that has equal appeal to both boys and girls and it's interesting how the book manages to balance an intricate and detailed love triangle with sequences of fairly gruesome violence. It's not often you find both these things between the covers of the same YA [young adult] book.

"It helps that Katniss Everdeen is extremely well-drawn; one of the reasons I liked the books so much. She's tough without being a tomboy and attractive without being a sophomore although she has elements of both. Her relationship with Peeta (is it love or expediency?) is particularly well-handled. Even she is unsure where her feelings truly lie."

Though Katniss, who is 16 in the first book, is buffeted by all the familiar teen emotions—the desire to be special competing with a wish to belong—Collins insists the series is not a metaphor for troubled adolescence. In a rare interview, with the US *School Library Journal*, she said: "I don't write about adolescence. I write about war for adolescents."

The Hunger Games' Adult Readership

Increasingly, though, adults are also reading *The Hunger Games*, which has been energetically marketed to the valuable crossover audience. Her UK publisher, Hilary Murray Hill, dates the tipping point back to 2010, when Collins was named one of *Time* magazine's 100 most influential people, and *Mockingjay*, the third volume in the trilogy, was published in both teen and adult editions. "We'd built the campaign around the books, rather than the author, and the excitement was very strong in the UK," she says.

There is a very grown-up political logic to the books, which become steadily more uncomfortable as they go on, ending with an ultra-dystopian society in which the rebels—Katniss among them—resort to the same power games as their one-time oppressors. "Panem is clearly the USA seen through a distorting mirror . . . with elements of the Roman empire thrown in. All very clever and thought-provoking," says Horowitz.

The writer Michael Rosen has written admiringly for the *Guardian* about the politics of Collins' dystopia. "What I thought was uplifting about *The Hunger Games* was that I was given plenty of clues of how power was enacted in this totalitarian future society—enough clues for me to see parallels in past and present political regimes. I felt I was being warned and I quite like being warned."

Rosen's article on the *Guardian*'s Comment Is Free website struck a geyser of opinion, ranging from those who accused it of political incoherence and wrongheaded moralism, to those who, like a user posting as "psygone", saw the trilogy as a projection of "the subconscious fears of today's teens that their future will be more and more grim, and they will have to do the 'unusual' in order to not be crushed by it".

Rosen feels the hostility was partly to do with readers' dislike of feeling manipulated. "Quite a few of the responses seemed to imply that other people were stupid if they liked it, or dangerously vulnerable to its subtle right-wing ideas. But I'm quite happy to be warned by literature—particularly if the writer has enabled you to 'get behind' the dystopia, giving you some sense of how it came about, or how it's structured. I thought *The Hunger Games* did precisely that."

An Unapologetic Author

Collins is unapologetic about the moral message of her books. She says: "I hope it does make people think about what they watch in a more reflective way." But she also points out that different readers relate to different themes in the books. "For some it's the violence and the reality TV; others seem to be affected by the themes of hunger—food is a power tool that runs throughout it. Other people seem to home right in on the romance. I don't think I've ever had a book or a television project where so much of the experience was dependent on the reader's own experience, and that's been really fun."

Julia Eccleshare, children's books editor of the *Guardian*, agrees that the power of the trilogy lies not so much in the writing as in the space it leaves for these different readings. "Adults see it as a depressing reflection of the terrible state the world is in, but young readers see it as full of potential and excitement. Katniss embodies the triumph of survival. She's stroppy, which we all are; beautiful, which we all want to be; and powerful, which you have to be in order to survive. It's Occupy meets Big Brother meets a bit of magic. Plus you MUST have friends, which is the 21st-century youth mantra."

So who reads it? [Hilary] Murray Hill says the fan base is pretty evenly spread between the sexes, highly unusual for books with female heroines. To this core readership, the film has added action movie fans and connoisseurs of political dystopias.

The whole phenomenon could be summed up in the familiar phrase, coined by the Romans used to describe their strategy for placating the plebeians—"bread and circuses". For all Collins' reluctance to play the media, her great good fortune is to live in an age when the movie circus can spread the bread of literature so widely. With two more films still to come, you can bet that irony isn't lost on her.

The Last Battle: With *Mockingjay* on Its Way, Suzanne Collins Weighs in on Katniss and the Capitol

Rick Margolis

Rick Margolis has served as the executive editor of School Library Journal.

Just before the publication of the last volume of The Hunger Games *trilogy, Mockingjay, editor Rick Margolis sat down for an interview with Suzanne Collins. Though Collins at the time would not reveal what would occur in the third book, joking that all she could say was that the cover was blue, she openly discussed myriad issues in the three books. Collins gives an insightful analysis of the mockingjay as a symbol for Katniss; talks about her background as a screenwriter and how it helped her write dialogue but hindered her as a descriptive writer; and gives insights into her family history that led her to become a writer of war novels for children. Finally, Collins avers that it is a desirable outcome if children have a better understanding of war through reading her books, and that, perhaps war, like American slavery, will one day be a thing of the past.*

The suspense is killing us. Ever since Katniss Everdeen, the arrow-slinging heroine of Suzanne Collins's *Hunger Games* trilogy, was snatched from the cruel clutches of a ruthless government, we can't stop thinking about the feisty 16-year-old from District 12. What sort of flesh-devouring, mutant-killing machine awaits her next? How can she possibly lead a successful revolt against the technologically advanced Capitol? And what about her two teen suitors—Gale, a longtime hunting buddy, and Peeta Mellark, the baker's selfless son? Which hunk will she finally choose? Ah, the questions are endless.

Lucky for us, we figured if we interviewed Collins, we'd get an advance copy of *Mockingjay*, the final book of the best-selling series. But we soon discovered that Scholastic had forgotten to mention one crucial thing: *Mockingjay* is embargoed—no exceptions, no siree, Bob! So no matter how hard we pleaded, we couldn't persuade the publisher to send us a copy before the national laydown date of August 24. And to make matters worse, we strongly suspected that Collins couldn't say much about the new book. Suddenly, the interview didn't seem like such a great idea.

But then we thought back to our first encounter with the Connecticut writer. It was August 2008, and even though *The Hunger Games* wouldn't be published for another month, it was already getting tons of buzz from bloggers and reviewers. Even *adult* book reviewers were getting into the act, including author Stephen King, who said he couldn't put the book down. It looked like Collins, a longtime scriptwriter for kids' TV shows such as *Wow! Wow! Wubbzy!* and the author of the five-part Underland Chronicles, had a crossover hit on her hands. And when we finally sat down with her, she turned out to be a total trouper: thoughtful, engaging, and surprisingly funny. And that's what ultimately convinced us to go ahead with this interview.

We thought, What the heck? Even if Collins can't talk about her upcoming blockbuster, she's bound to have some special insights about the series and its characters. And who knows? Maybe, just maybe, she'll let something slip about book three. . . .

We're like the odd couple. I haven't read the book, and you can't talk about it.

I was saying to my husband, "What am I going to say? They won't let him read the book. And, you know, it hasn't come out yet. And the film [Lionsgate acquired the film rights for *The Hunger Games* in 2009] is in such an early stage of development—it hasn't been green-lit—I don't have all this stuff to report about it. What am I going to say about the book?" And Cap said, "Tell him it's blue." [Laughter] So, OK, it's blue.

Did you have a particular shade in mind?

I can't say anything specific about the book. But I can say that I feel it is the story I set out to tell. I pitched the story as a trilogy, and thematically this is the place I was headed for in all three books. I really hope it speaks to the audience, that it makes them think and feel the things that I intended. And I'm really looking forward to talking to a group who's completed the trilogy. There's a lot I have not been able to discuss because it would tip off too much of the ending.

Since your upcoming book is called Mockingjay, *would you like to explain the origin of that species?*

Sure, absolutely. Back in Panem, in the Dark Days, which were 75 years ago when there was an act of rebellion going on in the country, the Capitol created this bird in its labs called the jabberjay. It was just this small black bird, and it had a crest. But it was genetically designed so that it essentially could record what it heard spoken. So they would send it into wooded areas where the rebels were, and it would record the dialogue. Then it would fly home and recite what it had heard.

Well, the rebels caught on to what was going on, and they started to feed the jabberjays false information. And at some point, the Capitol figured that out and left the jabberjays to their own in the wild, thinking they would simply die out. But instead, they mated with female mockingbirds, and this whole new species was created, which are the mockingjays.

Now the thing about the mockingjays is that they were never meant to be created. They were not a part of the Capitol's design. So here's this creature that the Capitol never meant to exist, and through the will of survival, this creature exists. And then it procreated, so there are now mockingjays all over the place.

What does that have to do with Katniss?

Symbolically, I suppose, Katniss is something like a mockingjay in and of herself. She is a girl who should never have existed. And the reason she does exist is that she comes from District 12, which is sort of the joke of the 12 districts of Panem. The Capitol is lax there. The security is much less. The peacekeepers, who are the peacekeeping force, are still the law, and they're still threatening, but they intermix more with the population in District 12 than they do in other districts. And also things like the fence that surrounds 12 isn't electrified full time.

Because of these lapses in security and the Capitol just thinking that 12 is not ever really going to be a threat because it's small and poor, they create an environment in which Katniss develops, in which she is created, this girl who slips under this fence, which isn't electrified, and learns to be a hunter. Not only that, she's a survivalist, and along with that goes a degree of independent thinking that is unusual in the districts.

So here we have her arriving in the arena in the first book, not only equipped as someone who can keep herself alive in this environment—and then once she gets the bow and arrows, can be lethal—but she's also somebody who already thinks outside the box because they just haven't been paying attention to District 12. So in that way, too, Katniss is the mockingjay. She is the thing that should never have been created, that the Capitol never intended to happen. In the same way they just let the jabberjays go and thought, "We don't have to worry about them," they thought, "We don't have to worry about District 12." And this new creature evolved, which is the mockingjay, which is Katniss.

That's a fascinating analysis.

Well, everything I just told you about Katniss is never really expressed in the books. I don't think anybody ever says what I just said. I'm just telling you the symbolic parallel there. Now you have an angle for your story.

Thank God!

Thank God! What were we going to do?

This is a minor point, but I'm curious: Why does President Snow's breath smell like blood?

Oh, I can't tell you that. [Laughter] I see what you're doing. You get me going, and then you have this list of book-three questions you're trying to slip in.

Who, me?

Do you think I can possibly answer that?

Actually, the entire interview has been carefully leading up to that very question.

[Laughter] Well, I absolutely cannot tell you. No, I really can't. But you're right. That will be answered in book three. I'll tell you that, OK? That can be your header.

Is this an SLJ [School Library Journal] *scoop?*

Yeah. [Laughter]

I just reread the first two Hunger Games *books, and it's a terrific story. But what really impressed me was how well it was written.*

Oh, thank you. I'm not very objective about that. You know, so much of my background is in scriptwriting, so I still feel very new to the book scene and writing prose. Prose is full of many challenges and unexplored territory for me because I came to it later in my life. Maybe it always feels that way for everybody, even if they started in prose in the beginning. But for me, so much of it has a brand-new or a "How do I do this?" feeling. I mean, I've written the five-part Gregor series and now three books with Katniss, and in neither series do I ever even leave the protagonist. I've never done multiple voices or viewpoints. There are just worlds of stuff for me to learn.

Is it easier for you to write dialogue than descriptive passages?

Oh, yeah. I've been doing scriptwriting for 27 years and books for maybe 10 years now. I think I started the first Gregor book, *Gregor the Overlander*, when I was 38. I'd be clicking along through dialogue and action sequences. That's fine, that's like stage directions. But whenever I hit a descriptive passage, it was like running into a wall. I remember particularly there's a moment early on when Gregor walks through this curtain of moths, and he gets his first look at the underground city of Regalia. So it's this descriptive scene of the city. Wow, did that take me a long time to write! And I went back and looked at it. It's just a couple of paragraphs. It killed me. It took forever.

Is it still a struggle for you to write those scenes?

As time has passed, descriptions come a little bit easier. Scripts are essentially dialogue and stage directions. And then you rely on your director, actors, and designers to bring so much physical and emotional detail to the story. But in a book, it's all up to you. I've finally accepted that no designer is going to step in and take care of the descriptive passages for me, so I've got to write them.

But here's the great thing about writing books as opposed to scriptwriting: There are no budget concerns. No one is ever going to tell you that they can't afford to build the set or to travel to a location or to do a special effect, and you're not going to write a scene that in your mind you set on the African veldt and there are herds of animals going by, and then, ultimately, you end up with one giraffe and one lion. [Laughter] That happened to me once in an animation. And they're like, "Suzanne, it's not *The Lion King*." And I'm like, "I know, I know, I just had this image...."

On a more serious note, your last eight novels have closely examined the effects of war and violence on children. Why are you so obsessed with that topic?

That would definitely go back to my childhood. My father was career Air Force. He was in the Air Force for 30-some years. He was also a Vietnam veteran. He was there the year I was six. Beyond that, though, he was a doctor of political science, a military specialist, and a historian; he was a very intelligent man. And he felt that it was part of his responsibility to teach us, his children, about history and war. When I think back, at the center of all this is the question of what makes a necessary war—at what point is it justifiable or unavoidable?

So let me get this straight. You're a young kid and your dad is discussing the philosophical significance of war with you and your three siblings?

Ab-so-lutely! One of my earliest memories is being at West Point and watching the cadets drill on the field. If you went to a battleground with my father, you would hear what led up to the battle. You would hear about the war. You would have the battle reenacted for you, I mean, verbally, and then the fallout from the battle.

And having been in a war himself and having come from a family in which he had a brother in World War II and a father in World War I, these were not distant or academic questions for him. They were, but they were also very personal questions for him. He would discuss these things at a level that he thought we could understand and were acceptable for our age. But, really, he thought a lot was acceptable for our age, and I approach my books in the same way.

How so?

I mean, a lot of things happen in Gregor. Those books are probably for—what?—ages 9 to 12 or 9 to 14? There's biological terrorism in the third book. There's genocide in the fourth book. There's a very graphic war in the fifth book. But I felt that if my audience came with me from the beginning of that series, they would be able to understand that in context. And I feel the same way about the *Hunger Games* series.

You know, I have two children of my own, so I can think about, "Alright, how would I say this to them?" Things were discussed with me at a very early age. For some people, both of these series, Gregor and *The Hunger Games*, are fantasies; some people call them sci-fi. But for me, they're absolutely, first and foremost, war stories.

One of the most disturbing aspects of The Hunger Games *is that children are forced to murder other children on live TV. I can't think of another series for young people that has so much kid-on-kid violence.*

Well, the thing is, whatever I write, whether it's for TV or whether it's books, even if I'm writing for preschoolers, I want the protagonist to be the age of the viewing audience. So I'm not going to write a war story for kids and then just have them on the sidelines. If I write a war story for kids, they're going to be the warriors in it.

And if it's a gladiator story—which is how *The Hunger Games* began, I'd say it's essentially a gladiator story—then the children are going to be the gladiators. They're not going to be sidelined. They're going to be the active participants in it. There will be adult characters, but you're going to go through it with someone who is the age of the intended audience.

Your books send a strong message that grown-ups have messed up the world big time, and kids are the only hope for the future.

Absolutely. I can't remember how much we talked about Theseus and the Minotaur the last time we spoke, but Theseus and the Minotaur is the classical setup for where *The Hunger Games* begins, you know, with the tale of Minos in Crete. . . .

Right. As punishment, Minos ordered the Athenians to throw seven young men and seven maidens into a labyrinth to be devoured by the Minotaur—until Theseus finally kills the monster. I remember you telling me that as an eight-year-old, you were horrified that Crete was so cruel—and that in her own way, Katniss is a futuristic Theseus.

But once *The Hunger Games* story takes off, I actually would say that the historical figure of Spartacus really becomes more of a model for the arc of the three books, for Katniss. We don't know a lot of details about his life, but there was this guy named Spartacus who was a gladiator who broke out of the arena and led a rebellion against an oppressive government that led to what is called the Third Servile War. He caused the Romans quite a bit of trouble. And, ultimately, he died.

What do you hope young readers take away from your books?

One of the reasons it's important for me to write about war is I really think that the concept of war, the specifics of war, the nature of war, the ethical ambiguities of war are introduced too late to children. I think they can hear them, understand them, know about them, at a much younger age without being scared to death by the stories. It's not comfortable for us to talk about, so we generally don't talk about these issues with our kids. But I feel that if the whole concept of war were introduced to kids at an earlier age, we would have better dialogues going on about it, and we would have a fuller understanding.

Can those dialogues help put an end to war?

Eventually, you hope. Obviously, we're not in a position at the moment for the eradication of war to seem like anything but a far-off dream. But at one time, the eradication of slave markets in the United States seemed very far off. I mean, people have to begin somewhere. We can change. We can evolve as a species. It's not simple, and it's a very long and drawn-out process, but you can hope.

The Hunger Games Changed Suzanne Collins's Life

Hillel Italie

Hillel Italie writes for the Associated Press.

Suzanne Collins knew her life had changed permanently when she began receiving telephone calls at her home from strangers and had to get an unlisted number. The daughter of a military man turned history professor, Collins was schooled in military history by her father and used this knowledge in her books. For years Collins worked in television, writing scripts for popular Nickelodeon shows, until one day her producer and friend suggested she write novels. Collins's first series was the Underland Chronicles, which, like The Hunger Games *trilogy, told a story about war. Collins believes that young people can understand the issues surrounding warfare at an early age and that they should not be sheltered from such knowledge.*

As she worked on the final book of her *Hunger Games* trilogy, Suzanne Collins discovered that her life had changed. "I started to get calls from people I didn't know, at my home number, which at the time was listed and we had never thought anything about it," says Collins, a 48-year-old mother of two who lives with her husband in rural Connecticut.

Collins the Celebrity

"Suddenly, there was this shift. Nothing threatening happened or anything, but it is your home and you want it to be private. So I think that was the point where I felt, 'Oh, something different is happening now.'"

Hillel Italie, "How Has 'Hunger Games' Author Suzanne Collins' Life Changed?," *Huffington Post*, September 23, 2010. Copyright © 2010 by Associated Press. All rights reserved. Reproduced by permission.

With the release of *Mockingjay*, an instant chart topper, Suzanne Collins is a celebrity. Perhaps not the kind you'd spot on the street, but one whose name is known and welcome to millions of readers, young adult and adult. Her fame comes not from wizards or vampires, but from her portrait of a brutish, dystopian future in which young people are forced to fight to the death, on television.

Inspiration, like a sudden phone call, began at home. A few years ago, Collins was surfing channels late at night and found herself switching between a reality program and news reports about the Iraq war. The images blurred in her mind. She wondered whether other viewers could tell them apart.

"We have so much programming coming at us all the time," she says. "Is it too much? Are we becoming desensitized to the entire experience? . . . I can't believe a certain amount of that isn't happening."

Narrated by the teenage rebel-heroine Katniss Everdeen, the *Hunger Games* books (*The Hunger Games, Catching Fire* and *Mockingjay*) fare also as stories of honor and courage in the worst of times, when, as Collins notes, honor and courage may be all you have. The stories begin with Katniss volunteering to stand in when her little sister is called to participate in the televised games, the "hunger games." She learns about love, too. A romantic triangle among Katniss and her noble suitors, Peeta and Gale, has divided readers into *Twilight*-like camps.

Drawing on Greek Mythology

Collins' sources run much deeper than television. She cites the Greek myth of Theseus and the Minotaur, in which seven boys and seven girls are sacrificed to keep Athens safe. She was also inspired by *Spartacus*, the epic film starring [American actor] Kirk Douglas as the rebellious Roman slave, and by the classical [Roman] biographer Plutarch. The stories are set in a country called Panem—in honor of the old Roman ex-

Author Suzanne Collins attends the Los Angeles premiere of the film adaptation of her book The Hunger Games *on March 12, 2012.* © Steve Granitz/WireImage/Getty Images.

pression for mindless diversion, *panem et circenses*, meaning bread and circuses, or bread and games.

"I have been following her for a long time. She is one of the authors who got my older son reading, so I owe her a personal debt on those grounds," says Rick Riordan, author of the million-selling Percy Jackson series and the upcoming Heroes of Olympus series, which also draw upon ancient Greek culture.

"I think she does a wonderful job of mixing good action, with strong characters, with a dash of humor and really providing readers everything they need to have a page-turning experience. She's just a masterful writer."

Collins was interviewed recently at the offices of [book publisher] Scholastic Inc., her long, blonde hair parted in the middle, wearing a pendant with the *Hunger Games* icon, a golden winged hybrid—a mockingjay—clutching an arrow in its beak. She has a careful, deliberate speaking style and a passion for explaining and clarifying subjects. She is a storyteller who wants her books not just to entertain, but to provoke. The young are her ideal readers.

"I think right now there's a distinct uneasiness in the country that the kids feel," Collins says, citing the economy and the wars in Iraq and Afghanistan. "Dystopian stories are places where you can play out the scenarios in your head—your anxieties—and see what might come of them. And, hopefully, as a young person, with the possibilities of the future waiting for you, you're thinking about how to head these things off."

Collins' Background

The daughter of a career Air Force officer, Collins lived all over the world as a child, from New York City to Brussels, and was reading Greek myths at an early age. Her father served in Vietnam and later taught history, not just to college students, but to his own family.

"I believe he felt a great responsibility and urgency about educating his children about war," she says. "He would take us frequently to places like battlefields and war monuments. It would start back with whatever had precipitated the war and moved up through the battlefield you were standing in and through that and after that. It was a very comprehensive tour guide experience. So throughout our lives we basically heard about war."

Collins graduated from Indiana University with a double major in theater and telecommunications, and received a master's in dramatic writing from New York University. She worked on several children's programs, including *Clarissa Explains It All* and *Little Bear*. Her work was noticed by *Generation O!* creator James Proimos, who hired her as head writer. They became good friends, and he suggested she try writing books.

A Gifted Writer

"She seemed like a book writer to me; it was sort of her personality. She also had the style and the mind of a novelist," says Proimos, who has written and illustrated several children's books. "I was telling her that you can't do TV forever; it's a young person's business. With books, at the very worst, you start out slow, but you can do them for the rest of your life."

Collins began working on what became her first series, the five-part Underland Chronicles. She liked the idea of taking the *Alice in Wonderland* story and giving it an urban setting, where you fell through a manhole instead of a rabbit hole. At Proimos' suggestion, Collins contacted his agent, Rosemary B. Stimola of the Stimola Literary Studio. After hearing a little about the author's planned book, Stimola suggested she turn in a sample chapter.

"Quite honestly, I knew from the very first paragraph I had a very gifted writer," says Stimola, who still represents Collins. "It happens like that sometimes. Not often, but when it does it's a thing of beauty. From the very first paragraph she established a character I cared about. She established a story and a mood that touched my heart."

Collins sees her books as variations of war stories. The Underland series, she explains, tells five different aspects of conflict—the rescue of a prisoner of war, an assassination, biological weapons, genocide and the use of military intelligence. *The Hunger Games* series is an exploration of "unnecessary" war and "necessary" war, when armed rebellion is the only choice.

"If we introduce kids to these ideas earlier, we could get a dialogue about war going earlier and possibly it would lead to more solutions," she says. "I just feel it isn't discussed, not the way it should be. I think that's because it's uncomfortable for people. It's not pleasant to talk about. I know from my experience that we are quite capable of understanding things and processing them at an early age."

Social Issues in Literature

CHAPTER 2

Violence in *The Hunger Games* Trilogy

The Hunger Games Taps into Adolescent Issues of Dating and Death

Brian Bethune

Brian Bethune is a senior writer and book reviewer for Maclean's, *a Canadian periodical. He has published articles on Canadian writers such as Margaret Atwood and Charles Taylor.*

In the following viewpoint, Bethune explores the landscape of contemporary young adult (YA) dystopian fiction, citing The Hunger Games *as the most successful in a long line of adult and YA novels about imperfect societies. Utopian fiction, depicting perfect worlds, used to be in fashion, Bethune writes, but the troubled modern world has given rise to many more fictional dystopian societies, and novels for teenagers reflect the turmoil of the world they see around them. A story in which children kill their peers is not so far-fetched to teenage girls who live in a vicious social milieu, Bethune suggests. There is a dark side to teenagers, and contemporary dystopian fiction by Collins and her peers only reflects the real world around us.*

Imagine a life where possibilities are opening at a speed that veers unpredictably between exhilarating and terrifying. The familiar, precisely because it's familiar and safe, still tugs at you, but even so, you want out because your old life constricts as much as it comforts. Besides, your social milieu, which often feels like an endless struggle to achieve, or resist being slotted into some arbitrary niches—pretty, ugly, smart, dumb, athlete, klutz—is changing fast. You feel driven—by inner need and outside pressure—to make choices. Meanwhile, the manipulative, often harsh, powers that be, who created the larger world they're busy shoving you into, have clearly not done a bang-up job of it, either in their personal lives or as part of society. And they want you to get out there and fix their mistakes—just at a moment when worry over the imminent demise of their entire socioeconomic structure is never far from the surface. It can be cruel and scary out there. Dystopian, even.

Chances are, anyone not imagining this life, but actually living it, is a teenager. And living it in an era of economic uncertainty, conspiracy theories and fear of environmental collapse. Western civilization used to produce literary utopias, but in the past century of world wars, financial panics, murderous totalitarian regimes and nuclear threat, dystopias have outnumbered sunny projections by several orders of magnitude. Pessimistic depictions of the future are now everywhere in popular culture. Teens and teen books are not immune to larger trends in society.

The Hunger Games Movie Phenomenon

Whether any given North American teen is familiar with the entire library of novels casting adolescent emotions and life against some rather disturbing backgrounds, he or she—particularly she—is certainly aware of *The Hunger Games*. The film version of the pop culture phenomenon, as metaphor-rich a teen dystopia as could be—high school–age kids put in an arena to literally kill each other for the amusement of grown-ups—set a record for a non-sequel on its March 23 [2012] opening day with $68.25 million in ticket sales. That was the fifth-best all-time opening day; three days later, after sales reached $155 million, the movie had the third-best opening weekend ever, and again, the non-sequel record. With advance sales also setting records, many screenings are fully booked for days to come.

Actress Jennifer Lawrence plays Katniss Everdeen in the screen adaptation of The Hunger Games. © AF archive/Alamy.

Aided by its strong male draw—audiences so far have been 40 per cent men, compared to the *Twilight* series' 20 per cent—*The Hunger Games* and its coming sequels seem likely to eclipse the total take of the blockbuster vampire-romance movies. Giant photos of Jennifer Lawrence, who plays heroine Katniss Everdeen, usually with bow and arrow in hand, are plastered everywhere. There's a *Hunger Games* board game, in which the action is not set during the actual death match—unlike video game makers, all-ages board game manufacturers shrink from scenarios which require players to slaughter their opponents—but during pre-games training. Other franchise tie-ins include a $14.95 lightbulb featuring a red mockingjay (a hybrid creature crucial to *The Hunger Games* storyline), knee socks, ear buds, a Barbie doll, a replica bow, and even girls' underwear that salute the baker's son who is one of Katniss's suitors: "Peeta: so sensitive . . . with great buns."

The anticipation of success pumped up the fortunes of Lionsgate, the Vancouver-founded entertainment company that made the film, even before it opened. Its stock price hit a 52-week high last week [in April 2012], closing at $14.55 a share, up 90 per cent for the year. . . . The studio is not the only entity cashing in. The state tourism agency in North Carolina, which provided the film's locations, is offering special hotel packages, as well as organizing reenactments of key scenes and survival skills courses. As happened in the town of Forks, Wash., the setting for *Twilight*, fans are arriving in enthusiastic packs, delighting local merchants.

Those who don't stand to make money are somewhat less happy. The owner of Henry River Mill Village, which served as Katniss's Appalachian home, sounded as exasperated as Jean-François L'Huilier, the mayor of Rennes le-Château in France did in 2004, when he felt forced to transfer the remains of [Roman Catholic priest] Abbe [François] Bérenger Saunière (1852–1917) into a fan-proof concrete grave after *The Da Vinci Code* [the film version of Dan Brown's novel] devotees descended upon the Pyrenean hamlet of 150 souls. "The tourists come here and stomp all over the place with no respect for anything or anyone," complained L'Huilier. "They set off explosions and climb over the cemetery wall to dig up the dead. That's why I had to exhume the corpse." Wade Shepherd, 83, the North Carolina village owner, hasn't had to cope with any explosions (yet), but the fans are coming already. "Day and night, they're driving through, taking pictures, getting out and walking. I'm just bombarded with people."

The Book

As was the case with [Stephenie Meyer's] *Twilight* and [Dan Brown's] *The Da Vinci Code, The Hunger Games* frenzy began with a book. Suzanne Collins's 2008 novel and its two sequels, *Catching Fire* (2009) and *Mockingjay* (2010), sold very well before the movie was announced. By late 2010 there were almost three million copies in print. Now there are 10 times as many, in 26 languages in 38 countries, including two million in

Canada. And the novels have been equally strong in e-book format—Collins was the first young adult genre author (and 6th author overall) to join Amazon's "Kindle Million Club," meaning she had sold over a million Kindle versions. Earlier this month she shot to the top of the list as Kindle's best-selling author ever.

Her success is hardly surprising. There can scarcely be anyone left in North America who doesn't know the basic outline of *The Hunger Games.* Katniss, 16, a coal miner's daughter whose father dies in a mine explosion before the story opens, lives in the poorest part of the poorest district (No. 12) of near-future Panem, a North American authoritarian state that rose from the ashes of ecological catastrophe—worsening climate, rising sea levels and resource wars. The residents of the ruling Capitol live in high-tech splendour, governing with an iron fist the 12 outlying districts. There were once 13 districts, but in the course of putting down a massive rebellion two generations before, the Capitol obliterated No. 13. Now, as part of the ongoing price the lords of Panem exact from their surviving subjects, the better to keep them in a state of terror and abject submission, each district annually sends a male child and a female child, aged 12–18, to fight in the Hunger Games until only one remains alive. Every moment of the games, from the actual killings to individual moments of despair, is televised. Viewing is compulsory in the districts and hugely popular in the Capitol, where the pampered inhabitants lay bets on the winner and often intervene by sponsoring the more appealing among the so-called tributes—that is, by providing timely gifts of food, weapons or medicine that can make the difference between life and death. That makes strategy as important as brute force or killing skills, and a young girl can win the games over older and stronger males.

Katniss is a highly compartmentalized character, focused on providing for her family, particularly her 12-year-old sister

Primrose, after her father dies and her mother becomes paralyzed with grief. Her relentless drive to protect her sister is why Katniss takes up illegal hunting, becoming a skilled archer in the process, and why, unlike her male poaching companion, 18-year-old Gale, she doesn't spend any time thinking about the political system that grinds down her and her neighbours. Or, for that matter, any time noticing Gale's romantic interest in her. And it's why, too, Katniss ends up in the 74th Hunger Games: after Prim is randomly chosen as District 12's female tribute, Katniss immediately volunteers to take her place. The male tribute picked is Peeta, also 16, also romantically inclined toward Katniss, who is, once again, utterly unaware of it. The two travel to the Capitol where, under the tutelage of Haymitch Abernathy, District 12's only living previous winner, they develop a strategy—genuine on Peeta's part, ambiguous at best on Katniss's—of attracting sponsors by playing star-crossed young lovers.

Violence in *The Hunger Games*

Small wonder *The Hunger Games* created a stir in 2008. With a well-written and even better-paced story, a not entirely likeable but hugely compelling lead character, a dash of romance (all the more interesting for its uncertainty), and a powerful major theme that taps into our fascination—and unease—with reality TV (particularly the intimate, purportedly behind-the-scenes parts), Collins's novel hit the zeitgeist [spirit of the age] dead on.

And then there's the aspect of it so large that many of its cheering fans seem unable to consciously see it—the children are killing each other in a battle for survival, as savage a satire of high school and our contemporary economic distemper as can be imagined. For its teen target audience, especially girls, who live in a social milieu potentially even more vicious than that of adolescent boys, it could scarcely offer more appeal.

Parents, though, are certainly conscious of the child-on-child violence, and for every individual who posts that it's never too soon for the youngsters to learn it's a Darwinian world out there—as if middle school hadn't already taught them that—or that "the game is rigged," as one jaundiced mother commented, many more are worried. Violence in movies that draw kids is always a concern, but killing of teens by other teens has led to media appearances by child psychologists discussing the potential effect on younger viewers and cultural critics weighing in more generally. YA [young adult] novelist Kenneth Oppel, given op-ed space in the [Canadian newspaper the] *Globe and Mail*, assumes Collins is crassly exploiting our culture's delight in violence as entertainment, before concluding that modern society is so twisted that volunteers would line up for a real Hunger Games, so long as the winner was guaranteed "the latest iPhone and a lifetime unlimited data plan"—a statement that exceeds the cynicism he ascribes to Collins. At least her characters are fighting for their lives.

The Dystopian Novel Genre

And *The Hunger Games* is hardly alone on the shelves of children's bookstores, which are packed with teen novels of wildly divergent plots but eerily similar themes. Young adult dystopia, broadly defined—tales for teens about survival in a world of cruel or helpless adults, where everything is falling apart and the competition for resources or safety can include turning on one another—is a literary genre whose time has come.

"I look up at the wall where we post our YA best sellers," says Phyllis Simon, co-owner of Vancouver's [bookstore] Kidsbooks, "and I can see that the top five or six are dystopias." Whether they are the classic form, featuring harshly repressive societies, or post-apocalyptic scenes of chaos—both neatly mirror the seesaw nature of teenage life—they almost all have the same root cause as *The Hunger Games*: climatic catastrophe. "There's no fuel, there's no water," Simon notes. Or, sometimes, there's too much. In Scottish writer Julie Bertagna's *Exodus*, first published in 2002 before the dystopia wave gathered force, and re-issued in February, it is 2099 and the world is drowning. As the polar ice melts and the seas rise, 15-year-old Mara and her family have to flee their fast-disappearing island for a city built on the drowned ruins of [the Scottish city of] Glasgow. But there is no true asylum in a high-tech city that rules with primitive force, and Mara has to find her people a new home.

In *The Way We Fall*, published in January, Toronto writer Megan Crewe moves her fast-paced story, set in an island community off Nova Scotia [in eastern Canada], from the here and now through a near-future apocalypse to the brink of a dystopia, all thanks to a killer virus. Crewe doesn't explain where the disease comes from, but lethal viruses, which terrify some people more than anything else—including Crewe, who began her novel "after a zombie virus story gave me a nightmare"—are almost never natural in origin. They are either the work of demented governments and hubristic scientists, or, in our era of migrating viruses, a subset of climate change apocalypses.

Popular Adult Dystopias

In these deep backgrounds, teen dystopias are in tune with their adult counterparts, whose worries have changed over time. *Brave New World* (1932) expressed author Aldous Huxley's contempt for a consumer society drugging itself into oblivion; [British novelist] William Golding's *Lord of the Flies* (1954), now taught to teens, was actually a postwar Freudian [after psychologist Sigmund Freud] allegory for adults about the porous line between civilization and savagery; [British novelist] George Orwell's *Nineteen Eighty-Four* (1949) and a host of others, like [American science fiction novelist] Ray

Bradbury's *Fahrenheit 451* (1953) warned of a totalitarian future; while *On the Beach*, [British novelist] Nevil Shute's post-nuclear-war best seller of 1957, captures the ultimate fear of the Cold War generation.

Lately, though, the world's nuclear terror has either been forgotten or become too familiar to trouble us anymore. It's now all climate change in adult fiction too, as in [Canadian novelist] Margaret Atwood's *Oryx and Crake*. In that 2003 book, her second dystopian novel (she also supplied the introduction to a 75th anniversary edition of *Brave New World*), Atwood fit in global warming, reckless science and a fatal virus. And it is adults, after all, who write the teen books, points out Canadian Moira Young, author of one of this season's hottest titles, *Blood Red Road*, about a teen girl who leaves her dust bowl home in search of her kidnapped twin brother. Today's YA dystopias are the work of adults "worried about the planet, the degradation of civil society and the bitter inheritance we're leaving the young."

The Dark Side of Teens

And they're happy to embrace it, laughs Simon. "There's a dark side to teens, you know. They love melodrama, they love big emotion—and what's bigger than the whole world going to hell because the adults have screwed up?" Teen literature, like teen lives, is a matter of firsts—"first love, first rebellion, first everything," says Melissa Bourdon-King, general manager of Mabel's Fables bookstore in Toronto. Nor do adolescents realize they are reprising the emotions, if not the circumstances, of their parents. "I was reading *The Day of the Triffids* and *Fahrenheit 451* in the 1960s when Detroit was burning," adds Mabel's owner Eleanor LeFave. "Do you think," she asks rhetorically, "that a renewed interest in dystopias might reflect the times?"

Still, the best, and the best-selling, of them do more than echo the headlines. As Megan Crewe points out: "The successful stories all marry exciting and frightening plot lines with more ordinary concerns that matter emotionally to teens— and their two main focuses are a love interest and what kind of person will I grow into." Dating and death, to exaggerate only slightly. On Crewe's plague island [setting of the novel], her own heroine, 16-year-old Kaelyn, is already concerned about her possible grown-up self, already realizing her parents in particular and adult society in general have feet of clay, be- fore the slow slide into anarchy and death—*The Way We Fall* is perfectly titled—forces everyone to make moral as well as pragmatic choices. "YA dystopias work not because teens think those actual events are going to happen—however plausible they may be—but because the real emotions they would evoke are caught. When I'm writing I try to remember how I felt as a teen. People who dismiss YA books have simply forgotten how complex they themselves were at that age."

Death and dating is one summation of *Battle Royale*, the 1999 Japanese novel that is one of the grandfathers of the genre and, for many, a direct inspiration for *The Hunger Games*. In Koushun Takami's story set in a near-future totali- tarian Japan, the government terrorizes the population by ran- domly choosing a high school class, isolating the students on an island, and forcing them to kill each other until only one remains. The crucial difference between their situation and the one in *The Hunger Games* is that Collins's tributes might know, among their opponents, only the other tribute from their district. *Battle Royale* involves a class full of teens who know each other well, with all the crushes, friendships and an- tagonisms that entails. If *The Hunger Games* is reality TV ratcheted to a madly logical end, *Battle Royale* is extreme high school: dating and death, indeed. . . .

[YA dystopian novels] are as much alike in their deep structure as they are varied on their surfaces. Their characters live, for the most part, in post-sexist societies; the protagonists are far more often female than in past adventure stories, and the girls all have kick-ass potential. Like Katniss, they rescue more than they are rescued. Even more remarkably, no one in the stories finds this startling—for all their other sins, in these dystopias gender equality has arrived. Often, at 16, 17 or 18, the young protagonists are forced to make a choice, a decision that will make them compete with their peers, force them into a niche, restrict their possibilities. Some resist from the beginning, while others are looking forward to their futures before an inadvertent peek behind the curtain of adult lies opens their eyes. They find their parents and teachers to be repressive or, more often, helpless; they are tossed, willy-nilly, into rebellion.

It's teenage life writ large in an era when the prevailing concept of the future is more gloomy than not. And it's written well, too, which is the real key to success. Teen dystopias, which always end more optimistically than their adult counterparts, are exciting and empowering stories. The stakes are usually very high indeed. Adults are the problem. And kids are the saviours. Of course the books are flying off the shelves.

Violence in *The Hunger Games* Is a Reflection of Our Own World

Rebecca Keegan

Rebecca Keegan writes for the Los Angeles Times. *She is the author of* The Futurist: The Life and Films of James Cameron.
Keegan notes that violence in works aimed at children is nothing new. Brutality has a long tradition in literature as an allegory for adult cruelty, a mirror of the turmoil of adolescence, or a device to raise the story's intensity. Keegan interviews Maria Tatar, professor of folklore and mythology at Harvard University, who states that Suzanne Collins is reminding the reader (and viewer) that such violence is "within us." The gory nature of The Hunger Games *follows in the tradition of such works as the Grimms' fairy tales and William Golding's* Lord of the Flies. *Between the ages of twelve and twenty-four, the brain is undergoing a radical transformation, and the turmoil of much young adult literature captures that confused state. Stories such as* The Hunger Games, *Keegan writes, can be cathartic, and adults as well as young people can find a spiritually useful connection in such literature.*

Children murder one another in a multitude of gruesome and memorable ways in *The Hunger Games*, deploying spears, arrows, rocks, venomous wasps, mutant wolves and their bare hands in a televised gladiatorial death match.

It Takes a Child

The juvenile slaughterfest depicted in the film and its source material, Suzanne Collins' trilogy of best-selling young adult novels, may give audiences (particularly parents) pause—is

Rebecca Keegan, "'Hunger Games': A Dark Mirror on Our Own World," *Los Angeles Times*, March 26, 2012. Copyright © 2012 Los Angeles Times. Reprinted with permission.

this what contemporary entertainment has come to? But violence committed by and against children has a long, grisly tradition in literature—as an allegory for adult cruelty, a representation of the emotional volatility of adolescence and a tension-raiser for audiences.

"We are eager voyeurs," said Maria Tatar, chair of the program in folklore and mythology at Harvard University and author of *Enchanted Hunters: The Power of Stories in Childhood.* "I start to question my own excitement about this movie. Why do I want to watch this? Why is it so seductive to see children in peril? The author is critiquing violence, but she's reminding us that we are implicated. It's within us."

Collins has said she found inspiration for her story, which is set in the future, in the ancient Greek myth of Theseus and the Minotaur, in which . . . Athens [was forced to] send seven boys and girls each year as food for the half-man, half-bull, until Theseus slays the beast. In *The Hunger Games*, Katniss Everdeen, a 16-year-old tomboy handy with a bow and arrow, is a Theseus-type character, a young savior fighting on behalf of all the other children.

"There's a part of us that feels that only a child can save us," Tatar said. "It takes the innocence and purity of a child. That fantasy has been around since before Christ."

Earlier Disturbing Literature

The brutality of the Hunger Games, which results in the deaths of more than 20 youths, follows in the gory footsteps of many of the Grimms' [referring to German folklorists Wilhelm and Jacob Grimm] fairy tales, which were first published in 1812. In "Hansel and Gretel," a pair of abandoned siblings escape from a cannibalistic witch by stuffing her into the oven; in "The Juniper Tree," a woman slams the lid of a trunk on her stepson and decapitates him; and in the axiomatically titled "How Some Children Played at Slaughtering," a little boy stands in for a pig in a child's game of butchering.

Often, stories of barbarous children are actually fables about the present-day behavior of adults. In William Golding's 1954 novel *Lord of the Flies*, a group of boys stuck on a deserted island descends into savagery, slaughtering and torturing one another in a bid for power.

"This is a dystopian nightmare in which [Golding] shows us our own culture," said John Granger, author of several literary analyses of the *Harry Potter* and *Twilight* books and editor of the bookish website HogwartsProfessor.com. "This was about 1950s conformity, that that conformity had a back to it as well as a front. Yes, we defeated the Nazis, but we continued to treat black people like animals. In backlash to that conformity, we get stories like *Lord of the Flies*. We get to see our own world in a very dark mirror. We can recognize ourselves in this very ugly reflection."

Embattled Children

From Oliver Twist to Harry Potter, many of literature's embattled children share a defining quality—the loss of at least one parent. In Katniss's case, her father is dead and her mother is emotionally absent.

"When you have a hero or heroine who's an orphan, you engage the reader's natural, protective sympathy," said Granger. "You have heightened the reader's experience. You identify with that young person."

The drama of the violent Hunger Games contest and Katniss's need to fight it on her own may appeal particularly to adolescents because they are going through a crucial stage of emotional development, according to child and adolescent psychiatrist Harold Koplewicz.

"Between the ages of 11 and 24, your brain is going through a remarkable revolution," said Koplewicz, president of the Child Mind Institute in New York. "Your emotional development is accelerated before your impulse control. You're freezing, you're boiling, you hate [everyone], you love them.

You have very deep and well-felt emotions, but it's very hard. The look of Hunger Games, of fighting for your life, of feeling like your parents are nowhere around, captures that."

For teens—for whom so much of life can feel like the end of the world—the post-apocalyptic terror of *The Hunger Games* and other stories about youngsters in battle can be cathartic. But for adults, there can be a spiritually useful connection as well.

"We are curious human beings," said Tatar. "We want to know, what if? What if we're faced with the worst possible scenario? What would we do to survive? That's what makes us human. Who wants to read about sunshine and happiness? I worry with the protagonist. I want her to survive. I want her to make it through, and I want to know how she did it because I want to be able to use that kind of knowledge and intelligence when I'm faced with something that feels impossible."

Love Is the Strongest Weapon in *The Hunger Games*

Mary Borsellino

Mary Borsellino's books include The Wolf House *series and* The Devil's Mixtape. *She lives in Melbourne, Australia.*

In the following viewpoint, Borsellino maintains that more than bombs, fire, arrows, or any of the other inventive weaponry used in The Hunger Games, *love is Katniss's most powerful weapon. Borsellino compares three totalitarian novels—Nineteen Eighty-Four,* V for Vendetta, *and* The Hunger Games—*to demonstrate that in a society where love is against the laws of those in control, love is a political act. Borsellino writes that Katniss—a hard, calculating, distrustful person—is most successful when she fights against the Capitol using the power of love as a form of rebellion. Katniss can survive and ultimately triumph over Snow and his minions because her heart is a weapon, and the way to keep fighting against the Capitol's horror and cruelty is by continuing to love.*

There's a piece of graffiti on a wall in Palestine. Over the years since it was painted, it's been photographed by scores of travelers and journalists. It reads:

> Your heart is a weapon the size of your fist. Keep fighting. Keep loving.

More than bombs, fire, guns or arrows, love is the most powerful weapon in *The Hunger Games*. It stirs and feeds the rebellion. It saves the doomed. It destroys the bereaved. And it gives even the most devastated survivors a reason to go on.

Mary Borsellino, "The Heart Is a Weapon the Size of Your Fist," in *The Girl Who Was on Fire: Your Favorite Authors on Suzanne Collins' Hunger Games Trilogy*, ed. Leah Wilson. BenBella Books, 2011, pp. 29–39. Copyright © 2011 by BenBella Books. All rights reserved. Reproduced by permission.

Love Survives

"Love" is not synonymous with "passion." Hatred is also a passionate emotion. When I say "love" here, I mean compassion, loyalty, empathy, and the bonds of friendship, family, and romance. All these things are present in Suzanne Collins' *The Hunger Games* series. So, too, are greed, selfishness, hatred, and fear. That the protagonists are able to put stock in love, even while given so many reasons to hate, is what gives *The Hunger Games* a note of hope despite the suffering of the characters.

The Hunger Games is part of a genre of post-apocalyptic political fiction, the best known example of which is [British author] George Orwell's *Nineteen Eighty-Four.* Suzanne Collins has said that *Nineteen Eighty-Four* is a book she reads over and over again, and *The Hunger Games* shows a great debt to Orwell's novel and to subsequent variations on it such as the graphic novel *V for Vendetta* [written by Alan Moore and illustrated by David Lloyd].

Both *The Hunger Games* and *Nineteen Eighty-Four* pit the power of hate versus the power of love. In *Nineteen Eighty-Four,* it's hate that ultimately triumphs, but *The Hunger Games*—which is American, as opposed to British, and so perhaps comes from a more culturally optimistic place when it comes to rebellions—ultimately insists that love is strong enough to survive through the horrors placed before it.

The Hunger Games' Katniss was a hard, calculating, distrustful person even before her time in the arenas and the war, and yet her largest decisions are always motivated by love. She volunteers for the games in order to save Prim's life, something that is almost never done because the Capitol teaches people to put their own self-preservation before any bond of love in such a situation, even a bond as close as that between Katniss and Prim. Katniss defies this.

Suzanne Collins has explained that Katniss is "a girl who should never have existed," an unexpected outcome of a secu-

Actresses Jennifer Lawrence and Willow Shields play Katniss and Prim Everdeen, respectively, in the screen adaptation of The Hunger Games. © *Moviestore Collection Ltd / Alamy.*

rity glitch in the Capitol's regime, just like the mockingjays. She is "this girl who slips under this fence ... and along with that goes a degree of independent thinking that is unusual in the districts."

Neither of the cages the Capitol has in place—the fence, prioritizing self-preservation over love for family or friends— hold her, and by breaking out, she makes other people realize that they can, too. On live television, all over Panem, she introduces a radical new idea: that it is important to care about other people; that it is the most important thing in the world.

Big Brother

While we're talking about television, it's important to touch on one of the strangest ways in which *The Hunger Games* owes a debt to *Nineteen Eighty-Four*. *Nineteen Eighty-Four* includes the phrase "Big Brother is watching you," which in that novel means that the state—personified by its leader, Big

Brother—can see everything you do. You are never safe from its surveillance, and all treason will be found out.

These days, of course, "Big Brother" means something completely different, as it is the name of one of the first of the wildly popular shows in the reality television genre. In *Big Brother*, a group of people are thrown together in a closed environment and watched by audiences at home. Big Brother is watching them, and we are watching *Big Brother*.

President Snow, in controlling the districts via the Hunger Games, is both Big Brothers at once: the dictator and the reality television producer. *The Hunger Games* series very consciously plays with the fact that it follows not only Orwell's novel, but also the entertainment revolution it inadvertently spawned.

In *Nineteen Eighty-Four* there is another equivalent to President Snow, a character named O'Brien who, in describing how his government has achieved such total power over people, also neatly sums up the Capitol's intentions:

> We have cut the links between child and parent, and between man and man, and between man and woman.

This is what makes Katniss' self-sacrifice for Prim such a powerful act. If the Capitol had really succeeded at severing those links, then it would have been Primrose Everdeen who went into the arena, not her older sister, wouldn't it?

And there is a love story in *Nineteen Eighty-Four*, just as there is one in *The Hunger Games*. In *Nineteen Eighty-Four*, it is between a man named Winston and a woman named Julia. Like Peeta in *Mockingjay*, Winston and Julia are punished for their rebellion by being tortured in specific ways that make them hate the person they were once in love with. Like Katniss, their wills are finally broken when they are presented with what, to them, is the worst thing in the world. (The worst thing for Katniss was losing Prim, but for Winston it is much more banal: He has a phobia of rats, and is threatened with being eaten by them. Julia's worst fear is never revealed to the reader.)

Love as a Rebellious Act

When the two love stories are compared, you can see much of Winston and Julia in the way Suzanne Collins has written Peeta and Katniss' story, and in just how important and powerful the romance Peeta and Katniss put on for the cameras through the first two novels of the trilogy is in stoking the flames of the rebellion.

In *Nineteen Eighty-Four*, Winston and Julia's love story starts when Julia slips Winston a piece of paper as they bump into one another one day.

> Whatever was written on the paper, it must have some kind of political meaning. . . . He flattened it out. On it was written, in a large unformed handwriting: I LOVE YOU.

If that sounds like a bait and switch—he expected something political, but really she's in love with him!—think again. Love when there isn't supposed to be love is a hugely subversive political act. If it weren't, there wouldn't be protest marches in countries all over the world demanding same-sex marriage. It was illegal until 1967 for black and white people to marry one another in some parts of the United States of America. A 2007 survey found that more than half of the Jewish people in Israel believed intermarriage between Jewish females and Arab males was equivalent to national treason.

When the love you feel is against the laws of those in control, then love is a political act. It's true in the real world, true in *Nineteen Eighty-Four*, and true in *The Hunger Games*.

When Katniss and Peeta make as if to kill themselves rather than one another at the end of the first games, it is seen by President Snow as dangerous because it could be interpreted as an act of rebellion. In *Catching Fire*, he demands that Katniss convince the districts that she acted out of love for Peeta, not out of defiance against the Capitol. As far as Snow can see, her actions are either/or—either Katniss looks like a rebel or she looks like a girl in love; her motivation can only be one or the other.

What President Snow never understands is that choosing love over survival is the ultimate act of defiance Katniss can make. It's not one or the other; the love and rebellion are one in the same.

Humanizing Actions

The Capitol teaches almost everyone to see the tributes as less than human: When Katniss is first being styled by her prep team, they wax and scrub her and then declare happily that she looks almost like a person. Before that, when Katniss says good-bye to Gale, he tells her that killing the other tributes won't be any different to killing animals in the woods. When President Snow's scientists hijack Peeta and make him think that Katniss is a mutt, it is only another example of the Capitol's commitment to dehumanization.

But Katniss doesn't accept that. She sees the value in human life, even as she is forced into becoming a killer and soldier. She teams up with Rue in the arena, rather than simply killing the little girl and taking out some of her competition. When Rue dies, Katniss sings to her, and covers her with flowers.

The effect of this tiny, humanizing act—singing to a dying child—has immediate and far-reaching consequences. Rue's district sends Katniss bread. Rue's fellow tribute spares her life when they face off later in the games. In *Catching Fire*, it's Rue's song that the district whistles to Katniss to show their support for her, and in *Mockingjay* Boggs offers Katniss' singing as a moment when he was touched by her.

Do you begin to see what President Snow couldn't?

Love, like fire, is catching.

Katniss, going along with Snow's plan to make the romance with Peeta seem to be the cause of her actions, can't see it either. But with every interview and appearance, she declares herself loyal to something other than the Capitol. And love has already proved to be more powerful than the Capitol, because both of District 12's tributes have survived the games.

V for Vendetta and The Hunger Games

Another post-apocalyptic political story of recent years was the graphic novel, and subsequent film, *V for Vendetta*. It, like *The Hunger Games*, is the story of the figurehead of a rebellion, and of a teenage girl, Evey. It, too, shows clear echoes of *Nineteen Eighty-Four* in its storytelling.

When Evey is captured by the police and taken to jail, she finds a letter hidden in her cell. It was from an earlier prisoner, Valerie, and tells the story of Valerie's life. Valerie was gay, rounded up and put to death in a concentration camp. In the letter left behind, she wrote:

> Our integrity sells for so little, but it is all we really have. It is the very last inch of us. . . . An inch, it is small and it is fragile, but it is the only thing in the world worth having. We must never lose it or give it away. We must never let them take it from us. . . . What I hope most of all is that you understand what I mean when I tell you that even though I do not know you, and even though I may never meet you, laugh with you, cry with you, or kiss you, I love you. With all my heart, I love you.

Valerie died because of who she loved, but her love is stronger than the hate that executed her. It survives her death, waiting patiently in the cell until Evey comes and finds it later.

Julia and Winston's love doesn't survive the things that they are put through when they are captured—the tortures hijack that last inch of them. When they see each other again, as broken and hijacked as Peeta becomes in *Mockingjay*, Winston thinks of an old song lyric:

Under the spreading chestnut tree

I sold you and you sold me.

The last time Katniss sees Peeta in the war, before trying to infiltrate Snow's mansion and instead witnessing the violent and horrific death of her sister, she imagines Gale being taken by peacekeepers and Peeta being forced to take the nightlock poison. She then thinks of "The Hanging Tree" song:

Are you, are you

Coming to the tree

Combined, the two songs become a question posed to Peeta and Katniss: Will fear, torture, hate, lust for power, and the desire for self-preservation ultimately prove to be so strong that even lovers would betray each other? Are they coming to the chestnut tree, where they will sell each other out?

The Hunger Games, however, declares that no, love *does* conquer hate, even in circumstances as dire as Katniss and Peeta's. Their love survives what Winston and Julia's cannot.

Katniss and Peeta both have moments of suicidal despair in *Mockingjay*. Peeta is tortured until he can't even remember what his favorite color is, much less whether or not he loves Katniss. Katniss loses Prim, the sister she loves more than her own life. They are broken as absolutely as Julia and Winston are broken.

But Katniss is driven by love and compassion, even when the thing she loves most in the world is dead. When President Coin asks the surviving tributes whether another Hunger Games should be held, Katniss understands that Coin is no different, in the end, than Snow. In order to ensure herself an opportunity to assassinate Coin, Katniss gives a vote of yes to the new round of games, and says that she does so "for Prim."

The explanation seems, on the surface, to be one of vengeance: For Prim's death, Katniss wants to see the children of the Capitol suffer in the same way. But in reality her motivation is self-sacrifice: Katniss began her journey when she put her own life in danger for Prim, for a child who would otherwise have died in the arena. Expecting to die after the assassination, Katniss once again places the life of children bound for the arena before her own by killing the woman who would have reinstated the games. And Katniss does so out of love—she does it for Prim, even if Prim is already dead.

Katniss remains true, even in the face of crushing loss and the prospect of her own death, to an ideal that Winston has in *Nineteen Eighty-Four* but is ultimately unable to uphold himself: "the object was not to stay alive but to stay human." Katniss retains that last inch of integrity and love that Valerie of *V for Vendetta* prized above life.

Love as Weakness and Strength

This is not to say that the power of love is always a triumphant force in *The Hunger Games*. Katniss' mother is a skilled healer who can face terrible injury and illness without flinching, but losing her husband almost killed her and, because she was incapable of caring for them in her depressed state, almost killed her daughters as well. Prim's death hits her so hard that she cannot be there for Katniss in the aftermath.

Love is the greatest strength any of the characters have going for them, but is also their greatest weakness. President Snow was able to coerce Finnick into sexual slavery by threatening to hurt those that Finnick loved if he didn't comply.

Yet the alternative—to have nobody you love—is infinitely worse than being made vulnerable by love. Johanna Mason explains in *Catching Fire* that there is nobody left whom she loves, and that this renders the jabberjays in the arena unable to hurt her through mimicking screams, though her meltdown during training in *Mockingjay* shows that even someone who loves nobody can still be wounded terribly by the Capitol.

When Peeta and Katniss are each wounded, just as deeply as Johanna, they have the other there to help them on the slow and rocky path to recovery. Johanna is no less damaged for her lack of love, but she doesn't have anyone to help her back afterwards.

Like Johanna, neither Snow nor Coin indicate at any point in *The Hunger Games* that there is anyone or anything that they themselves love. But both think that they understand what a powerful force love is, and both do their best to wield this power for their own evil ends.

In each case, however, their efforts backfire: By making Katniss emphasize her love story in *Catching Fire*, Snow does more to incite the rebellion against his Capitol than Katniss could have achieved on her own. And Coin, in attempting to reinstate the Hunger Games as a method of offering revenge to the districts, seals the death warrant on her regime and herself. The woman who views marriage as a reassignment of living quarters cannot anticipate the steadfast core of Katniss' compassion. Neither she nor Snow ever really understand love at all.

The Rebirth of Love

So what can we take from the stories of Winston and Julia, of Valerie, of Katniss and Peeta? Why does George Orwell end his love story with the lovers broken and defeated? Why does writer Alan Moore kill off the defiant Valerie? And, with these grim precedents in place, why does Suzanne Collins then decide to give Katniss and Peeta a fragile, scarred, but undeniably happy ending?

The answer may come from the connection Peeta and Katniss share to the land of District 12. The first time Katniss sees Peeta again, he is gardening, and it is the fearlessness Katniss feels in the wild that allowed her to survive her first trip to the arena. Katniss and Peeta are both linked to the natural world, and in the natural world even the worst of winters is followed by a spring.

The epilogue of *Mockingjay* shows Katniss watching her children play in the meadow, now green and lush once again. New life grows, even in graveyards. Rue's funeral song is able to become a child's simple tune once more. There are losses to mourn, but also children to love: Prim and her mother have both left Katniss forever, a discarded knitting basket remaining as a reminder, but Greasy Sae's granddaughter is there to take the wool instead.

Katniss and Peeta are both terribly scarred, physically and psychologically, by their experiences in the arenas and the war. But they are able to go on, and survive the pain. Katniss describes the way she copes with her moments of terror and pain: "I make a list in my head of every act of goodness I've seen someone do."

Katniss Everdeen can survive her darkness because she understands the same truth that's expressed in that graffiti in Palestine. Her heart is a weapon, and the way to keep fighting against all the horror and cruelty of the world is to wield that weapon. To keep loving.

Katniss Becomes a Killer Kid

Lois H. Gresh

Lois H. Gresh is a New York Times *best-selling author of sixteen science and popular culture books and eight science fiction novels. Among her works are* The Twilight Companion: The Unauthorized Guide to the Series *and* The Science of Stephen King.

Gresh discusses the phenomenon of child soldiers in the following viewpoint. When Katniss becomes first a killer in The Hunger Games *and* Catching Fire, *and later, a child soldier in* Mockingjay, *she is following in a tradition of child warriors around the world, not only in historical times, but also in contemporary society. Katniss undergoes an evolution from a girl who struggles mightily with the notion of killing others to the cold-blooded murderer who shoots down other tributes, and ultimately, President Coin. The effects of being a child warrior are long-lasting, and Katniss, like other young soldiers, does not escape unscarred. As* Mockingjay *winds down, Gresh writes, Katniss struggles with suicidal thoughts, drug addiction, and other clear signs of post-traumatic stress disorder.*

"The awful thing is that if I can forget they're people, it will be no different at all [from killing animals]." So thinks Katniss in *The Hunger Games.*

This statement occurs very early in the three-book series, and in many ways, it is a premonition of what is to come. In times of war, as discussed a bit in the previous chapter, soldiers may start to view the enemy as nothing more than objects. They are the "others," no more human than a bug. In times of religious combat, such as during the Crusades or anywhere in the world today where terrorism occurs, the kill-

Lois H. Gresh, "Killer Kids: How Responsible Are They?," *Guide to the Hunger Games*, St. Martin's Griffin: 2011, pp. 169–177. Copyright © 2011 by Macmillan. All rights reserved. Reproduced by permission.

ers tend to forget that they are indeed murdering *human be-ings*. Children on one side of a border are no different from those on the other side: Both are living, breathing, thinking human beings. But as soldiers, crusaders, and terrorists grow more accustomed to acts of cruelty and killing, they slide into automatic pilot mode, and killing humans becomes no different from killing animals.

Katniss the Killing Machine

Katniss's evolution into a killing machine takes time. At first, she kills animals so her family won't starve. Her first solo hunt results in supplying a rabbit to her hungry mother and sister. She's killing for the same reason animals hunt in the wild: to survive. She doesn't know it at the time, but soon, she'll be forced to hunt and kill humans for the same reason: to survive.

In her first Hunger Games, she must kill other children in order to save her own life. The first person she kills—ever, in her entire life—is a boy who spears her friend Rue. After shooting an arrow into the boy's neck, she wonders why she even cares about his death. She has already evolved from a girl who had to learn how to hunt animals for food to someone capable of murder. And while, yes, eventually she would have to kill the boy anyway to become the winning tribute, she kills him without thinking in a cold act of retaliation. She's angry that Rue is dead, and she wants him to pay.

Somehow, the reader empathizes with her and is pleased when she kills the boy who took poor Rue's life. Even we, the readers who are not in combat at all, understand why Katniss has killed another person. In fact, we identify so strongly with Katniss that we want her to emerge from the games as the victor, and we know this means she must kill multiple children. We see Rue's murderer as "evil" and we see no reason why Katniss shouldn't do away with him and save her own neck.

Child soldiers exist worldwide. In this image, Free Syrian Army's young fighters pose on April 2, 2013, as they hold positions near the front line during clashes with regime forces in the old city of Aleppo. © Guillaume Briquet/AFP//Getty Images.

Even after her cold act of retribution, she identifies with the dead boy and those who mourn for him. She is not a killer at heart. Not yet.

By the time Katniss is in the thick of battle in the second book, she thinks like a killer: "I make a silent promise to return and finish [Beetee] off if I can." And by the time she leads the revolution in the third book, she blames herself for the hideous deaths of a lot of her companions, and worse, she is directly responsible for killing an "unarmed citizen."

How do people like Katniss and Peeta become killer kids? What makes a sweet, innocent child turn to murder?

Clearly, Katniss and Peeta must kill in order to remain alive. But Katniss herself comments more than once that she's become a killing machine, a killer, someone who actually mows down an unarmed woman. At what point does a *child* shift from killing for survival to killing *out of habit*?

Killer Kids

We've all seen photos of children holding machine guns with caps pulled low over their too-old eyes. The pictures are jarring because we don't associate the innocence of children with the evil of mass murder. Who puts deadly weapons into the hands of their young and sends them out to slay victims? Well, we know the Capitol and their gamemakers do it, but in the real world, leaders have been doing the same thing since the dawn of time. . . .

There's something profoundly disturbing about the idea of killer kids, whether in Hunger Games arenas, in the ancient gladiator battles, or in adult warfare. Humanitarians claim that it should be a war crime for adults to enlist children in warfare. They argue that innocent, vulnerable children are manipulated and lured into service and given lightweight weapons that turn them into killing machines. While this is true to some extent, it's not entirely true. Take Katniss Everdeen as a fictional example of what is also true in the real world. In *Mockingjay*, Katniss leads a rebellion because it is the only recourse the people have to find freedom. Though she resists the role for a long time, in the end, she takes on the leadership. A posse of adult generals doesn't show up in her town, kidnap her, and brainwash her to bear lightweight weapons and slaughter hundreds of innocent people. She rebels and fights against the posse of adults who have enslaved and tortured her people since the Dark Days. . . .

Western societies have . . . sent their children to war for centuries. In the middle ages, the British military included a lot of boys, and by the late nineteenth century, British institutions systematically recruited them. In 1803, the Duke of York founded the Royal Military Asylum to train boys as soldiers who might be able to lead others in battle. In 1765, Britain created the Royal Hibernian Military School from an orphanage to train twelve-year-old boys to serve as rank-and-file soldiers. In fact, these young Hibernian boys fought for the British during the American Revolution.

In the United States during the Civil War, boys routinely fought and died. Conservative estimates place the number of young boys battling for both the Union and Confederacy at approximately 250,000–420,000. Parents inducted them into service, as did schools. Many of them volunteered. Avery Brown enrolled in the military at the age of eight, lying on the recruitment paper that he was twelve, old enough to serve! John Clem enrolled at the age of ten, and his weapons of choice were a musket and a gun. Often called the "boys' war," the boy soldiers in the Civil War accounted for as much as 20 percent of all recruits.

Rather than consider it a crime that the boys served in war, the public at large considered their deaths noble; they were admired and respected.

Modern Child Warriors

Only in modern times and in the West, do we see the rising abhorrence by the public of sending children to war. This is, in large part, a reason why *The Hunger Games* trilogy strikes such a chord with readers. The modern Western reader thinks, *How can they send these boys and girls into battle? This is inhumane and against everything that's right!* But in reality, we've been doing it forever.

During the Industrial Revolution, it became more common to think of children as innocent youth who must be educated and protected, isolated from adults, and allowed to enjoy their childhoods for as long as possible. Formal schooling took hold and started replacing apprenticeship as the primary tool of education. Of course, many kids never made it through the formal education process. Many were orphans, many were poor. They were needed in coal mines, on farms, in factories, so they became warriors of another fashion: fighting the Industrial Revolution rather than a bloodbath war.

And along with the formal education came military disciplinary structure. To this day, military training is considered virtuous, and parents send their sons into the military to teach them discipline and morals and to provide structure to their lives. During the Industrial Revolution, uniforms and regimentation seeped into the schools, and off the children went to become officers and soldiers.

During World War I, the practice of enlisting boys continued. There were age restrictions, but still, it wasn't all that uncommon to find young boys fighting alongside men on the front lines.

In modern times, throughout the world, adults still view warrior children as honorable and moral, to be admired and respected. While the West may frown upon the practice and exclude its own young boys from combat, this idea is not globally accepted.

Killer kids are on the rise because the techniques of global warfare are changing. In 1996, Graça Machel wrote a landmark publication, *Impact of Armed Conflict on Children*, for the United Nations about this problem. The widow of Samora Machel, leader of the Mozambique guerrilla war against Portugal and first president of Mozambique, Graça Machel served as a guerrilla fighter in Tanzania and also fought against Portugal. She also served as minister of education for Mozambique and is famous worldwide as the wife of [South African leader] Nelson Mandela. In her report, she states that modern warfare has abandoned all standards of conduct due to the fact that globalization and revolution have decimated traditional societies. The breakdown in what was once normal societal structures has been exacerbated by governmental collapses, internal feuding, financial inequities, and the dissolution of services that are essential to life; among other factors. As everything normal collapses around people, civilians become warriors, and violence escalates. According to Machel, the horrors of modern combat that are now taken as givens include ethnic cleansing, genocide, systematic rapes, and the use of children in military combat.

Forced into Battle

As mentioned above, many children are forced into battle, such as in *The Hunger Games* trilogy. If they don't fight, they and/or their families are tortured and sometimes killed. To alienate new recruits, adults force the children to kill family members, neighbors, and friends. According to Amnesty International:

> Worldwide, hundreds of thousands of children under 18 have been affected by armed conflict. They are recruited into government armed forces, paramilitaries, civil militia and a variety of other armed groups. Often they are abducted at school, on the streets or at home. Others enlist "voluntarily," usually because they see few alternatives. Yet international law prohibits the participation in armed conflict of children aged under 18.

The figures are staggering. According to Peter W. Singer of the Brookings Institution, *before the war in Iraq*:

> Although there is global consensus against the morality of sending children into battle, this terrible practice is now a regular facet of contemporary warfare. There are some 300,000 children under the age of 18 (both boys and girls) presently serving as combatants around the globe, fighting in approximately 75% of the world's conflicts.

The United Nations wrote in 2000 that more than fifty countries were actively recruiting children into military service that year, and further, that the youngest known soldiers were only seven years old. Possibly even more grim, in the 1990s according to the United Nations, *2 million children were killed in armed combat; 4 to 5 million were disabled; 12 million were left homeless; and a staggering 10 million were "psychologically traumatized."*

Unfortunately, the use of killer kids isn't confined to fictional worlds. What brings it close and up front in the world of *The Hunger Games* is that we feel the atrocities in a very personal way—from the viewpoint of Katniss. We may be shocked by the real-world statistics, but the impact hits home when we read Katniss's story.

Let's look at a few real-world examples of child soldiers. First, there's the war in Iraq, where children are regularly recruited into military service. Saddam Hussein's government enlisted and trained thousands of children as young as ten years old. According to Singer:

> A common means for totalitarian regimes to maintain control is to set their country on a constant war footing and militarize society. This justifies heavy hierarchic control and helps divert internal tensions towards external foes. The recruitment, training, and indoctrination of children also offers the regime the opportunity to deepen its reach into Iraqi society.

Remind you of anything, say, the Capitol and its leaders in *The Hunger Games*? It's common practice for totalitarian regimes to keep civilians under control by maintaining an environment of constant threat of war. Sure, the Dark Days were seventy-five years ago and well into the past, but to maintain its grip on the population, the government saturates its propaganda with the idea that war could erupt again at any time. In addition, they prohibit districts from communicating with each other. They pit children against each other in the Hunger Games to maintain even tighter control over the people.

But Iraq is just one of hundreds of examples of child soldiers. . . .

Child Volunteers

Consider the Basij, a volunteer army founded by the Ayatollah Khomeini [in Iran] in 1975. People, including children and women, join the Basij for benefits and out of loyalty. The Student Basij is comprised of children who are in middle school and high school. They feel that they are holy martyrs, and during the Iran-Iraq War, tens of thousands of the Basij sacrificed their lives on the battlefield for the cause. Children and teenagers formed a battlefront line that moved constantly toward the enemy forces. As bullets, canons, and land mines mowed them down, more children and teenagers moved forward in additional suicidal lines. According to some reports, the Ayatollah Khomeini once said that "a country with twenty million youths must have twenty million riflemen or a military with twenty million soldiers; such a country will never be destroyed." And after the election of President Mahmoud Ahmadinejad in 2005, the government used the Basij to suppress possible rebellion. The same thing was done during the elections in 2009. In December 2009, thousands of middle and high school children fought to suppress student demonstrations—*yes, thousands of child soldiers battled other children on the streets of their own cities.*

How different are the Career Tributes, really, from the Basij and other children dedicated to fighting to the death for spiritual and political reasons? The Careers are volunteers in the Hunger Games, and train "throughout their lives" for the event. According to Katniss, they "project arrogance and brutality" and "head straight for the deadliest-looking weapons." Just as the Basij fight together, the Careers fight in packs against other tributes in the games.

Katniss, of course, is not a Career Tribute. She's forced into the Hunger Games like the Darfur children were forced into battle. She has no choice.

But later, as she hardens to acts of violence and murder, she becomes more of a volunteer. When she accepts the mantle of Mockingjay and leads the rebellion against the evil Capitol, her mind-set is more in the mode of the Basij than that of the naïve Katniss we saw in both *The Hunger Games* and *Catching Fire*. By the time she's in charge of Squad 451, she wants to be on the front lines.

Earlier, during her first games, she is almost killed by Thresh, but gets out of it by explaining how she sang to Rue as the little girl died. Poor Thresh is stricken, as most kids would be, with grief over the loss of Rue and also by gratitude to the girl who loved her as a sister. In a tragic error of judgment (for Thresh, certainly not for Katniss), he lets Katniss go out of respect for what she did for Rue. This seems highly unlikely, to be honest, but we can only assume that Thresh holds little value in his own life, that he's traumatized, and possibly, that he's not too sharp.

Later, Katniss is relieved to learn that Thresh has been killed by another tribute. Now, she won't be burdened by the dilemma of what to do should the two of them be forced to fight for their lives. Had she faced the identical dilemma in *Mockingjay*, after she'd hardened more to the thought of killing people, she might not have reacted in the same way. Instead, she might have had no qualms whatsoever about killing Thresh. But we'll never know because he dies in *The Hunger Games*.

Katniss's Evolution

Even Peeta sees how Katniss is changing over time. . . . Sometimes, they work together, as in killing Cato during their first games. Here, she's working *with* him, not against him, and she's killing with great regret and only because she has no choice if she's to survive. He's doing the same thing.

Sometimes, she thinks he's out to kill her, but then he begs her to kill him so she may live, which totally confuses her. She swings back and forth about Peeta, whether she trusts him, and whether she loves or fears him. It's common for people to swing back and forth, wondering about their boyfriends, girlfriends, and spouses. Love? Hate? The most passionate teenage lovers often end up breaking up for reasons they don't even understand. And it's not limited to teenagers. Adults who have been married for a long time and have children together break up far too frequently, as well, and they rarely understand the true reasons, either. Luckily, most of us don't have to thrust our romances into the horrors of a killing arena, where we have to wonder whether our potential mates are out to kill us or save us.

By the end of *Catching Fire*, Katniss kills other tributes, hoping their deaths will save Peeta. No wonder poor Peeta's confused. It's tough to understand why he is so kind to her in face of her often brutal treatment of him. How many guys hang in there, trying to win a girl's heart, when she keeps stringing him along, wondering if she's in love with somebody else? How many guys would put up with it—making their intentions to marry and love forever clear, making their utter devotion clear, while the girl isn't sure how she feels about some *other* guy? Toss the entire killing concept into the mix, and it's explosive. Does she want to kill him? This goes *far* beyond the question, *Will she ever love him?* But on the other hand, Peeta subjects Katniss to far more complex emotions: After all, he ends up thinking she's a nonhuman mutt who should be killed! No wonder poor Katniss is confused. He sums things up well when he tells her, "These last couple of years must have been exhausting for you. Trying to decide whether to kill me or not."

Eventually, Boggs wants Katniss to kill Peeta. Luckily, she still has enough self-control and remains Katniss of *The Hunger Games* at heart. She remains moral and decent.

Nonetheless, one of her conditions for taking on the role of Mockingjay is that she gets to kill President Snow. At this point, the reader figures she's now a killing machine as contrasted to the earlier Katniss we saw in *The Hunger Games.*

When in charge of Squad 451, not only does she want to be on the front lines, she's determined to kill Snow. Much to the shock of the reader, she votes "yes" for the symbolic Hunger Games that will pit Capitol children against each other. . . . Katniss probably votes "yes" as a ploy to push President Coin into thinking that she is on her side. This way, Coin will be easier for Katniss to assassinate. Katniss may be a killing machine at this point, but she retains her core personality: She does not really advocate another Hunger Games. Rather, she wants to get rid of Coin, who is as deplorable as Snow.

Given the same circumstances, many of us might do the same thing.

The Saddest Victims of Conflict

War and battle do crazy things to people. We've all heard about post-traumatic stress syndrome, for example, in which battle-weary soldiers become depressed, can't sleep, can't function, and don't think normally anymore. They are transformed by war into people who barely resemble the soldiers who left home before the battle.

Clearly, Katniss's suicidal tendencies and drug addiction as *Mockingjay* winds down are evidence of something akin to post-traumatic stress syndrome. She's lost the will to live. She's lost the ability to view herself as anything more than a terrible person. She takes drugs to zone herself out so she doesn't have to remember who she's killed and what she's done. Contrasted to her innate bravery and determination—she is a very strong person—she cannot live through war without breaking down in the end. She's traumatized to the point of total numbness.

Her behavior is very common for child soldiers, as described by the United Nations:

> Child soldiers are among the saddest victims of conflict: They rarely emerge from military service with a sense of their own worth and identity. Worse, they often experience violence that leaves them physically or psychologically scarred. Facing a difficult adolescence, many turn to drugs, alcohol and anti-social behaviour.

Indicting Violence:
A Pacifist Review of *The Hunger Games* Trilogy

Marty Troyer

Marty Troyer is pastor at the Houston Mennonite Church. He uses the sobriquet "The Peace Pastor." His online blog reaches an audience of tens of thousands of people.

Troyer examines The Hunger Games *trilogy from a pacifist perspective in the following viewpoint. He believes that Suzanne Collins's portrayal of violence is an indictment of such behavior and takes two major forms in the novels. The first is dominant violence, used by the Capitol to keep the districts in control. The second form is resistant violence, depicted when the districts fight back in* Mockingjay. *Though Troyer understands why the districts must engage in hostilities, no form of violence is acceptable to a pacifist, and he suggests that resistant violence can often evolve into dominant violence, as when President Coin proposes a new Hunger Games at the end of the novel to avenge the Capitol's long oppression of the districts. Violence only leads to more violence, Troyer asserts. When Katniss kills Coin, she finally ends the cycle of violence. However, the trilogy ends only with a cessation of warlike activities, Troyer argues. There is no real spirituality or insight into what might usher in a better world.*

Welcome to *The Hunger Games*, a trilogy dripping with the weight of oppression and the dread of liberation! Suzanne Collins has woven a fascinating tale for young and old alike that unpacks the complexity and devastation of war.

She's also given us a story for our times: the liberation of a people brutally oppressed by a privileged minority. Ultraviolent throughout, Collins' books are not on the surface pacifist. But this peace advocate absolutely loved the books and recommends you read them. Why? Because it's an honest look at the roots and limits of violence. Her indictment of violence by portraying violence is an enormous gift.

The Genesis of Violence

Let's start where Collins does, by passing judgment on violence's defensive or protectionary function. Like all good fiction, she doesn't tell you she's indicting violence, she invites you to feel the indictment through outrage, hate, betrayal, fear, despair, and manipulation. Your blood will boil along with every young adult reader as she unmasks dominant violence: violence used by dominant culture to protect itself. Set in the future of a post-American country called Panem, the Capitol wields absolute control over twelve outlying districts they violently subdue. In the name of security, Panem demands the annual sacrifice from each district of two innocent "tributes" who fight to the death in a survivor-like game called the Hunger Games. These teenage scapegoats pacify the districts (through fear) and leave the capital population feeling righteous, superior, and safe. Dominant violence—whether in daily life or the artificial setting of the games—is justified because it offers protection.

Collins says absolutely nothing positive about this form or function of dominant violence. The disconnect between the lavishness of life in the Capitol and the grotesqueness of death in the arena underscores how far we're willing to go to ignore the consequences of injustice in our world. Shirley Jackson, the author of a similar 1948 story called "The Lottery," said she wrote to "shock the story's readers with a graphic dramatization of the pointless violence and general inhumanity in their own lives." Collins does the same. Reminding us security must not trump justice, and that no amount of distance protects us from complicity.

When the security function morphs into oppression a new form of violence is born: resistant or revolutionary violence. This secondary violence is always, as theologian John Dear says, a response to dominant culture. Exploring liberation theology he says, "It starts with the inhuman experience of poverty, the institutionalized violence of misery which kills millions of people around the planet. It declares that the violence of poverty is not the will of God, that God wants every human being to have life to the full, not to die in misery. Liberation theology declares that God is actively involved in the struggles of the poor, to end the violence of poverty around the world."

It's possible to read the trilogy as a full-on support of resistant violence, given how well she differentiates between dominant and resistant violence. She clearly flips the script on which of the two is morally suspect. In my context (instigators of dominant violence and sometimes victims of resistance violence) and as a pacifist, this was terribly meaningful. When dominant cultures manipulate and disenfranchise minority communities, liberating movements have erupted throughout history. As one white woman learned after intentionally moving into the margins of Oakland,

> It is at least slightly easier, now, for me to identify with people who are disenfranchised [in multiple ways]—by race, poverty, social class, lack of access to education, constant threat of violence and humiliation, and more—and who suffer the worst effects of a violent and exploitative network of social and economic systems. I see the police brutality. I see the impossibility of navigating through even those social safety net programs that exist. I see the near futility of trying to thrive under these circumstances.

This is the story of the civil rights movement in the American South, with its tension between choosing violence or non-violence as the best response to white oppressive supremacy. As Martin Luther King Jr. said, "Riots grow out of intolerable conditions. Violent revolts are generated by revolting conditions." Peeta's bread (a gift of charity) is not enough to overcome such revolting conditions.

Collins helps you feel the conundrum of resistant violence as the grinding toll of injustice on selfhood and community. In the face of overwhelming might, horrifying genetic manipulation, and lack of a future, violence finds a foothold. She humanizes minority, gang, and third world violence by allowing us to feel the hope of freedom in the districts. Writing from the margins rather than from the center, she mirrors the biblical story without conjuring its religion. Dear says, "From Exodus to Isaiah, from the Gospel of Matthew to the Book of Revelation, we read about a God who takes sides with the poor in their struggle for liberation."

The Limits of Violence

Over and again *The Hunger Games* conjures hope through one of the core tools of resistance movements: symbol. Indeed, not just for plot turns, but in power, Collins' use of symbol overshadows the usefulness of violence. We see it everywhere: subverting imperial manipulation by eating berries à la *Romeo and Juliet*, decorating Rue's dead body and giving her the District 12 salute (along with District 7's response in kind), bread from District 7, Katniss' fiery dresses, the effigy of Seneca Crane, and of course the Mockingjay.

The power of symbol stands in contrast to the limits of violence in the story. A key scene from *Catching Fire* is Katniss' and Peeta's visit to District 7 where minority symbol and dominant violence are in tension, sparking revolution. Notice how symbol creates and spreads energy, whereas violence subdues it. It's also worth noting the extreme limits of violence, proven by the vibrant presence of a revolution in the face of overwhelming force!

Never does the author hail a military victory, and battles themselves are either glossed over or mentioned in fast form. Instead, what we get is the slow, painful unmasking of the games themselves, the awful effects of violence, and of the conditions in the districts. The widespread dissemination of that information becomes the key to revolution at a much higher level than violence. Change hinges on acceptance of reality from those with and without power.

The Effects of Violence

But nowhere does *The Hunger Games* indict violence more thoroughly than in unmasking the effects it has on both victim and perpetrator. Collins addresses this at both the corporate and individual level. Corporately, you have poverty and a welfare mentality on one hand, and extreme excess and disconnection on the other. Personally, the effect on perpetrators is to leave us soul-less and business-like, such as the "Careers" and President Coin (and the hundreds of Christians in Germany [during WWII] who "just followed orders").

The portrayal of descent into severe post-traumatic stress disorder (PTSD) is nothing short of brilliant. Peeta clinging to the back of a chair to will himself to leave violence on the battlefield and not at home. Finnick's overwhelming confusion. Katniss, hiding in closets and "losing" entire days. Indeed, I'm not sure I've ever read a work of popular fiction with a protagonist as thick as Katniss. Capable hero, confused lover, disloyal friend, vulnerable as both victim and perpetrator. Her pain becomes unbearable at the point where she becomes unable to differentiate between violence done to and by her. Hers is a psyche manipulated as much or more than Peeta's, though no tracker jacker venom was needed. And fittingly her—and the trilogy's—story comes to a sad and lifeless end.

The End of Violence

But not until she deals one last blow to violence. In *Mockingjay*, Katniss realizes two essential things: She was manipulated as much by District 13 as she had been by the Capitol, and that violence is cyclical and will continue unless someone stops it. Thus her final act of aggression is not to condemn one person among many, but the system of violence itself. In shooting the wrong president at close range, she unmasks the truth that violence only begets violence, killing the system. Note how Katniss actually verbally agrees that the new nation should continue the Hunger Games, at least for one year for punitive reasons. But do they? No! With her final arrow comes a permanent end to the games.

Gene Sharp is an expert in stopping cycles of violence. Sharp is not a moralist but a pragmatist, who bases his claims on an empirical analysis of history. He asserts that violence, even in the service of a just cause, often results in more problems than it solves, leading in turn to greater injustice and suffering; hence, the best way to oppose an unjust regime is through nonviolent action. Indeed, Bishop Oscar Romero said, "There is an unshakable moral principle that says one cannot do evil in order to achieve good." Revolutionary violence only serves to replace one despot for another. One only needs to look to Africa and Soviet Russia for several stunning examples of how easily resistant violence can be transformed into dominant violence.

In the final analysis, Collins offers us little beyond a sturdy "No!" to violence, leaving us hungering for a strategy and lifestyle to say "Yes" to. What's missing is a prophetic imagination. She leaves at least the following to her rabid fans to explore: the genuine power of nonviolent resistance, the World Peace Game, and practices of reconciliation such as the Truth and Reconciliation Commission of [South] Africa that promote movement for peoples who have been mutually destructive. She offers little hope beyond perseverance, no spirituality outside public ritual, and little insight into the world as it should be. Instead, what we get is a masterful look at the end of violence: the world as it is.

Glamour of Evil or Glimmer of Hope?

Patrick O'Hannigan

Patrick O'Hannigan lives in North Carolina and writes for the American Spectator.

Writing from a Christian perspective, O'Hannigan neverthe-less disagrees with fellow Christians who have found The Hun-ger Games *trilogy shallow, brutal, or misguided. O'Hannigan writes that controversy has dogged Collins's books because of the disturbing premise of children killing children, but that the books meet the traditional criterion for art: that readers must get something uplifting from it. O'Hannigan notes an absence of Christian names among the characters in the novel and states that in a world without a religious overlay, a barbaric event such as the Hunger Games is not surprising. Noting the trilogy's satiric intentions, O'Hannigan suggests that readers must view* The Hunger Games *in the same manner as other famous satiric dystopias including* Brave New World *and* Fahrenheit 451. *Collins does not advocate brutality, but critiques the savage society she created in a subtle and insightful manner.*

Suzanne Collins bottled lightning in writing her *Hunger Games* trilogy. Now that reviewers beyond the work's origi-nal young adult demographic have greeted the new movie based on the first book of that trilogy with varying degrees of enthusiasm, we who care about what influences us and our progeny have work of our own to do: We need to ask whether *The Hunger Games* franchise is worthwhile, or merely contrib-utes to the coarsening of culture that Collins' defenders say she has written a parable about.

Controversy dogs *The Hunger Games* because its fictional world of the not-too-distant future depends on a disturbing premise: In what used to be North America, a postwar dictatorship with a well-scrubbed capital city, an unbridled consumerist ethos, and a perverse sense of "Must See TV" now requires boy and girl gladiators chosen by lottery from formerly rebellious outlying territories to kill each other in annual games where winning brings financial rewards to one gladiator and his or her home district, but losing means death. There are no consolation prizes.

The main thread of the story follows Katniss and Peeta, contestants from an impoverished coal mining region. Peeta becomes a gladiator in the usual way (bad luck), but Katniss takes an unconventional route to the arena by volunteering to replace her younger and softer sister, who is too obviously vulnerable in her first year of lottery eligibility at age 12.

What thinkers from antiquity through the Renaissance would have said about a setup like this, we already know. Assuming for the sake of Western civilization that it is still appropriate to require something uplifting from art, thoughtful critics have to ask if *The Hunger Games* meets that criterion. I think it does.

Misgivings about what Suzanne Collins created do not always come from expected directions. Sister Helena Burns, member of a Catholic religious congregation whose mission (they call it a "charism") is to evangelize the world for Christ through the media, ended her review of the movie by calling it "extremely well done on all counts," and deferring to parental judgment about who should see it: "Once you know what you (and your children) are in for at the cinema, it's your call," she demurred.

Fortunately for the continued relevance of faith-based reviewing, other Christians did a better job of exploring moral issues in *The Hunger Games*. Working separately from similar perspectives, Fr. Robert Barron and movie critic Steven Greydanus cited a conspicuous lack of Christian influence as key to the Hunger Games environment. "I would argue that what keeps human sacrifice at bay is none other than Christianity, is this great religion that says 'no scapegoating violence'," Fr. Barron suggested, clearly hoping that *The Hunger Games* might help some people to see that.

Greydanus, meanwhile, read subtle purpose into the names that Collins gives her characters. Those names are botanical (Katniss, Willow) or Roman (Cato, Caesar, Cinna, Claudius, Seneca), he said. He is right about that, but would have done well to add a third ("Dickensian") category [after English novelist Charles Dickens], because "Effie Trinket," "Peeta Mellark," and "Haymitch Abernathy" are every bit as memorable as [Dickens characters] Uriah Heep and Martin Chuzzlewit were. In any event, Greydanus observed, "Christian names are almost completely absent, which makes sense, because in no culture with any lingering Christian influence could something quite as barbaric as the Hunger Games exist." Importantly for my point here, both Fr. Barron and Mr. Greydanus also thought that author Suzanne Collins and movie director Gary Ross had managed to create something unusually thought-provoking.

Why Collins chose to speculate about a world without Christianity is a question only she can answer definitively, but I suspect there is a clue in the title of an old blues song called "How Can I Miss You When You Won't Go Away?" You do not need to embrace Christianity to believe that barbarism would probably take center stage in its absence.

Writing for the prosecution, bookstore manager Clare Cannon offered an argument to the effect that there are five good reasons to decry the desensitizing or corrosive influence of *The Hunger Games*. Hers may be the most eloquent of the Christian misgivings about what Collins created. Without objecting to dystopian visions as such, Cannon charges Collins with advancing false notions of mercy as weakness, admiring cynicism, embracing unacknowledged hypocrisy, obscuring moral culpability, and lingering too lovingly over violence.

That five-point indictment must be taken seriously, although space constraints recast serious consideration as "a fair trial, followed by a first-class hanging"—which, come to think of it, is precisely what Ms. Cannon attempted while slamming *The Hunger Games.* Her argument would have been more convincing had it not suffered from overreach (about which more in a minute) and narrow focus.

Katniss Everdeen is *The Hunger Games* character who most compels our attention, and while Katniss is a resourceful young woman who loves her sister, she is also cynical, manipulative, confused, and hypocritical. Cannon understands that skill with a bow and arrow does not make anyone a paragon of virtue, but she ignores the fact that Collins also created the character of Peeta, who is simpler and more introspective than his fellow contestant. In the movie and the book, it is Peeta who first calls attention from within the narrative to how dehumanizing the games are, by expressing a hope that they not turn him into something he is not. Peeta can be deceitful, but what guile he has is used to protect Katniss because—as we quickly find out—he has a long-standing crush on her. Surprisingly, perhaps, self-preservation as an end in itself is not what motivates either of the lead characters. Supporting characters like Rue (youngest of the unwilling gladiators), Haymitch (mentor to spotlighted contestants), Caesar (compromising TV host), and Gale (friend left behind) also have unexpected layers. By emphasizing the shortcomings of one character, Cannon ignored the contrasting virtues of other characters.

The other problem with the Cannon indictment is that it is too ambitious. Anyone who doubts that need only read to the end of it, where Ms. Cannon recommends such alternatives to *The Hunger Games* as [Dutch Christian who rescued Jews during the Holocaust] Corrie ten Boom's *The Hiding*

Place and [Rwandan author] Immaculée Ilibagiza's *Left to Tell*. The ten Boom and Ilibagiza books are indeed excellent and rife with heroism, but the dire events in their pages really happened, and it is no part of honest criticism to hold fiction and nonfiction to the same standard. We ought instead to compare Collins with her novelist peers. Do the people who think Collins wrote a satirical failure also believe that [British novelist] Aldous Huxley was cheering for a new normal that included "pneumatic" women in *Brave New World*, or [American science fiction writer] Ray Bradbury was serious about the purported advantages of having firemen *start* fires in *Fahrenheit 451*?

Let's not forget that mortal combat between a teenager and an adult was central to the Harry Potter books, yet the death match there and in B-level films like [director Dan Bradley's] *Red Dawn* did not get as much attention because it was not institutionalized as a tool of repressive government or staged for entertainment.

Suzanne Collins grapples more directly than some of her peers have done with morally hazardous material, but grapple she does, and we should applaud her seriousness. Although *The Hunger Games* franchise is no substitute for a well-formed conscience, the work deserves better than critical dismissal. Ironically, the kids are alright.

The Hunger Games Distorts the Reality of War

Paul K. Chappell

Paul K. Chappell graduated from West Point in 2002. He served in the army for seven years, was deployed to Baghdad in 2006, and left active duty in November 2009 as a captain. He is the author of Will War Ever End?, The End of War, Peaceful Revolution, *and* The Art of Waging Peace. *He lives in Santa Barbara, California, and serves as peace leadership director for the Nuclear Age Peace Foundation.*

While conceding that he is only referencing the first book in The Hunger Games *trilogy, Chappell finds fault with Suzanne Collins's depiction of battle. As a former combat soldier, he maintains that Collins distorts reality, ignoring how soldiers often lose their composure completely during warfare and go berserk. Collins's tributes, only teenagers, should not be expected to retain their ability to fight to the death in a confined enclosure when a high percentage of braver, fully grown soldiers have fallen apart mentally in real battle scenarios. Chappell feels the need to undermine the truthfulness of* The Hunger Games *because it is taught in schools. Although he believes that few authors are ever honest about war, he cites Homer's* The Iliad *and J.R.R. Tolkien's* The Lord of the Rings *as two works that deal more truthfully with the horrors of battle.*

Seventeenth-century philosopher Thomas Hobbes had a negative view of human nature, leading many people to believe we are natural killers. Because of Hobbes, many people assume human beings in the "state of nature" were clubbing each other over the head in a violent free-for-all. Hobbes said that early humans were "in that condition which is called War; and such a war, as is of every man, against every man ... where every man is Enemy to every man ... and the life of man, *solitary* [emphasis added], poor, nasty, brutish, and short." But military history shows that when untrained human beings must face lethal combat alone as solitary individuals they usually fall apart mentally. Consequently, Hobbes' view of human nature is not only negative but unrealistic, because he did not study military history, human psychology, or anthropology ([anthropology professor] Douglas Fry's book *Beyond War* offers thorough anthropological evidence that early humans rarely killed each other).

Not Suitable for School

In addition to countering the myth that human beings are naturally violent, I am writing about *The Hunger Games* and contrasting it with the reality of war for several other reasons. One reason is because a seventh-grade teacher told me her students were reading the first book in *The Hunger Games* series in class and asked me to provide some thoughts that could sharpen their critical-thinking skills. Furthermore, *The Hunger Games* is now being used as required reading in many middle and high school classes around the country. This got my attention, because when students are required to read a book in school they have a reasonable expectation of being educated. If students are reading a book in school that grossly misrepresents very serious issues such as war, violence, and trauma, it is the responsibility not only of teachers but citizens as a whole to provide the students with accurate information, because the fate and survival of our country and planet depend on an educated and informed population.

But can inaccurate depictions of war, violence, and trauma really cause any harm, or are these misrepresentations mostly harmless? War, violence, and trauma destroy millions of lives, and whenever serious issues that destroy so many lives are depicted in inaccurate ways that neglect their real psychological harm, the results can be damaging. What if serious issues such as racism, sexism, drug addiction, rape, and slavery were depicted in grossly inaccurate ways that neglected their real psychological harm? And what if these misrepresentations were then brought into a classroom where students have a reasonable expectation of being educated?

Distorting Battle Trauma

A major problem with inaccurately depicting violence is that these misrepresentations tend to glamorize violence, war, and killing. Lieutenant Colonel Dave Grossman [author of *On Killing*] tells us: "*The American Soldier*, the official study of the performance of U.S. troops in World War II, tells of one survey in which a quarter of all U.S. soldiers in World War II admitted that they had lost control of their bladders, and an eighth of them admitted to defecating in their pants. If we look only at the individuals at the 'tip of the spear' and factor out those who did not experience intense combat, we can estimate that approximately 50 percent of those who did see intense combat admitted they had wet their pants and nearly 25 percent admitted they had messed themselves. Those are the ones who admitted it, so the actual number is probably higher, though we cannot know by how much. One veteran told me, 'Hell, Colonel, all that proves is that three out of four were damned liars!' That is probably unfair and inaccurate, but the reality is that the humiliation and social stigma associated with 'crapping yourself' probably results in many individuals being unwilling to admit the truth. 'I will go see a war movie,' said one Vietnam veteran, 'when the main character is shown shitting his pants in the battle scene.' Have you ever seen a movie that depicted a soldier defecating in his drawers in combat?"

Think about it. Have you ever seen an action movie where the hero urinates or defecates in his pants? Ever? The first book in *The Hunger Games* series also heavily distorts the reality of war trauma—commonly referred to as post-traumatic stress disorder [PTSD]. Many people think war trauma only takes effect after combat, not realizing that soldiers can collapse mentally *during* combat. The main character in *The Hunger Games* goes through therapy in the later books, but children reading the first book are given the unrealistic impression that our minds are virtually immune to trauma *during* combat. I have not read the other books, and I am focusing only on the first book because it is the one most commonly used in schools. Too often, war trauma is either presented in a shallow way (as it is in the first book of *The Hunger Games* series), or veterans are stereotyped as being "damaged goods." Both misrepresentations are inaccurate and dangerous. The most common features of serious war trauma are a chronic sense of meaninglessness, losing the will to live, mental breakdowns, an inability to trust that leads to self-destructive behavior, and going berserk. Jonathan Shay calls going berserk "the most important and distinctive element of combat trauma," and it can cause people to mutilate corpses and commit other atrocities.

War Trauma in *The Iliad*

If teachers do not give their students accurate information about war, violence, and trauma, some of the students reading *The Hunger Games* in school may think, "None of the children in *The Hunger Games* have mental breakdowns in combat, so I don't see why soldiers in war have so many problems." The situation in *The Hunger Games* is so extreme that at least some of the children would experience serious war trauma and have mental breakdowns during or even prior to the battle. In *The Iliad*, composed by Homer around three thousand years ago, the highly trained Greek warrior Achilles suf-

Actress Jennifer Lawrence plays Katniss Everdeen in the 2012 screen adaptation of The Hunger Games. © AF archive / Alamy.

fers from serious war trauma *during* the war. [Doctor and clinical psychiatrist] Jonathan Shay explains: "Profound grief and suicidal longing take hold of Achilles; he feels that he is already dead; he is tortured by guilt and the conviction that he should have died rather than his friend; he renounces all desire to return home alive; he goes berserk and commits atrocities against the living and the dead. This *is* the story of Achilles in *The Iliad.*"

Berserker Rage

It might seem like the children in *The Hunger Games* do not break down mentally because they still have a minuscule chance of surviving if they take the right actions, and unlike the terminal illness scenario, this gives them some control over their fate. But military history shows that when soldiers have a miniscule chance of surviving they are more likely to lose the will to live and become suicidal. This is why it is so important for military commanders to encourage their soldiers, give them hope, and maintain high morale. Most human beings want to have a reasonable level of control over their lives, and losing almost complete control can cause some people to believe the only control they have left is the decision to take their own lives.

When soldiers have almost no chance of surviving and are pushed to the breaking point they can also go berserk. This is why [Chinese author] Sun Tzu—who wrote *The Art of War* over two thousand years ago—advised military commanders to never trap their opponents into a corner, but to always give them an escape route because berserking soldiers are extremely dangerous. There is no indication in the first book of *The Hunger Games* series that any of the characters go berserk, because they always seem to act rationally. Common characteristics of berserker rage are suicidal behavior (because the person going berserk feels invincible), a severe lack of self-control that resembles intoxication, and the mutilation of corpses. The author makes a vague reference to participants in past events eating each other's hearts, but it is unclear whether this is a reference to berserker rage.

When books are used in schools they must be held to a higher standard. [Harper Lee's] *To Kill a Mockingbird* is taught in schools because it provides an accurate commentary on racism, but what if the book instead grossly misrepresented the harm caused by racism and segregation? Violence has become so normalized and glamorized in our society that depictions of violence are rarely assessed for their accuracy, but when the United States is involved in multiple wars overseas and American soldiers are returning home with physical and psychological wounds, we must seriously question what students are being taught about war, violence, and trauma.

Haymitch and PTSD

Several people have suggested to me that the first book does in fact teach students about war, violence, and trauma, because the "Hunger Games veteran" Haymitch—who won the competition when he was younger and serves as a mentor to the main character—is an alcoholic. But if he really has war trauma, why is his alcoholism always portrayed in a comical and harmless way in the first book? Haymitch seems like the stereotypical "alcoholic war veteran," except that his drunken antics come across as clownish. My father had severe war trauma from the Korean and Vietnam wars, and his violent rages were truly terrifying. If Haymitch is supposed to represent the effects of war trauma, students who read the book in school are given the impression that war trauma looks funny, rather than frightening.

People have also suggested to me that Haymitch is less affected by war trauma because he—like most of the other competitors in *The Hunger Games*—came from poverty. But do the poor value their lives less than the rich? My father, who was half white and half black, grew up under segregation in the South during the Great Depression. Many of the World War II and Korean War veterans also lived in poverty during the Great Depression. And soldiers throughout history did not have the luxuries we enjoy in the twenty-first century, while many were poor. So military history gives us overwhelming evidence that coming from poverty does not make people immune to war trauma.

Perhaps *The Hunger Games* is a blessing in disguise, because it can give students an opportunity to think critically and discuss serious issues such as war, violence, and trauma. *The Hunger Games* also has several noble themes and offers some useful critiques on society. I am not analyzing the writing quality, character development, or any part of the book other than its depiction of violence—one of its central themes. I don't think Suzanne Collins, the author of *The Hunger Games*, had any bad intentions or intentionally misrepresented war, violence, and trauma. There are many reasons to believe she tried to make the book as serious and realistic as possible. For example, she describes injuries in gory detail, and she explains physical adversities such as thirst and hunger with impressive thoroughness. But like many people in our society who have been misled by the myths of war, she has emphasized the physical adversity of war but greatly underestimated the psychological adversity. Inaccurate depictions of violence have been around for a long time, but *The Hunger Games* is unique because it distorts the psychological reality of war, violence, and trauma more than any book I have ever seen used in school.

The Lord of the Rings on War

For example, [J.R.R. Tolkien's] *The Lord of the Rings* trilogy has been around for over fifty years, and although it glosses over many aspects of war, it portrays war and violence far more realistically than *The Hunger Games*. In *The Lord of the Rings*, the ability of soldiers to fight courageously is more believable because they have reliable comrades, reliable leaders, and have had military training. Furthermore, killing monsters that don't look like us is less psychologically stressful than killing our own species, and this is why war propaganda often portrays the enemy as inhuman monsters. And although the hobbits aren't highly trained in combat, their ability to fight ferociously is believable because they are trying to protect their friends who are in immediate danger. I am certainly not saying *The Lord of the Rings* portrays war or trauma accurately. Instead, I am saying *The Hunger Games* is unique, because it is far more unrealistic than *The Lord of the Rings* and many other violent depictions in the past.

The Hunger Games is also unique because it is being taught in schools during a critical time in history when the destructive capacity of nuclear weapons makes war a threat to human survival. During this critical time in history it has never been more important for people to understand the reality of war.

Governments Perpetrate Violence in Contemporary Fictions

James Warner

James Warner is the author of All Her Father's Guns, *a novel published in 2011 by Numina Press. His short stories have appeared in many publications.*

In the following viewpoint, Warner first compares The Hunger Games *with a similar Japanese novel, Koushun Takami's* Battle Royale, *in which children are also forced to fight against and kill one another. Warner suggests that in both these novels, government is the evil force at work. Warner then compares both novels to William Golding's* Lord of the Flies, *the famous post–World War II novel in which boys stranded on an island devolve into savages. For Golding, evil is innate in humanity and is unleashed when the boys are trapped in a world without adult supervision. For Collins and Takami, conversely, the children must fight against the evils of adult oppression. The difference in the books reflects Japanese and American society, Warner suggests: In Japan, rules are not to be questioned. In the United States, an adolescent like Katniss can subvert authority. Warner concludes by wondering why people today are more trusting of the individual and skeptical toward governments. Are readers less naïve, or just naïve in a new way, he asks.*

In Suzanne Collins's *The Hunger Games*, the government places children aged between twelve and eighteen in an arena where they're required to kill each other. While Collins has said *The Hunger Games* was inspired by switching channels between reality TV and the Iraq war, her book feels more deeply indebted to the Vietnam War, in which her father went to serve when she was six. Besides the mountainous and wooded terrain where the fighting occurs, the features of *The Hunger Games* that especially evoke Vietnam are the use of a lottery to select contestants—Vietnam was the last U.S. war in which a draft lottery was used—and the scale of the unrest the games provokes—no U.S. war since the draft ended has inspired mass political protest on a comparable scale. By showing blue-collar people sacrificing their families while the elite and the media pontificate condescendingly and foolishly, the book taps into emotions about war that are still playing out in U.S. political culture. District 12 in *The Hunger Games* is an Appalachian mining area where memories linger of an uprising put down many generations before, much as real Appalachians recall the U.S. Civil War.

The Hunger Games is very well-plotted, and is also impressive for the sheer number of adolescent girl fantasies the heroine Katniss gets to fulfill: She saves her sister's life, goes to the big city and gets a free makeover, appears on TV in designer clothes as the star of a parade, teams with a boy who has had a long-term secret crush on her, gets to kill a privileged mean girl from a larger clique, and experiences her first kiss. Almost every conceivable PG-13 fantasy is covered, including even faking a love pact suicide on TV and, in the sequels, igniting a revolution through sheer personal charisma. Meanwhile Katniss is fulfilling what we see today as the duty of every adolescent—to see through the hypocrisy of her society and figure out how it really works—while forming alliances, competing, surviving, climbing trees, and even losing weight.

The Hunger Games and *Battle Royale*

Books that combine the power of anti-government rage and teen popularity anxiety are rare enough that the commercial success of *The Hunger Games* has brought renewed attention to [Japanese author] Koushun Takami's 1999 novel *Battle Royale*, a novel set on an island, under a government that selects a class of school children each year to fight each other to the death. This novel's historical resonance is with the tail end of World War Two, when the Japanese defended various islands to the last man. In an interview published in recent editions of the novel, Takami recalls his mother saying of World War Two, "We were against the war, but we just couldn't say it." From observations of a parent's experience, Takami and Collins each derived a deep-seated mistrust of how governments behave in wartime, and independently hatched similar plot scenarios.

The main difference between Japanese and U.S. society that comes across between the two books is that Takami sees it as hopeless to try and change the system, since in Japan drastic political change has only ever been imposed from above—Takami also says in his interview, "I wanted to write about the trapped feeling of living in Japan I've felt clearly since childhood—at the very least, from middle school on— and that's what I attempted to do. Here in Japan . . . even if a rule is clearly ridiculous, nobody will speak out against it. . . ." Collins on the other hand holds the more American belief that one can use the media to subvert the power structure. According to *The Hunger Games*, there can be a revolution precisely as long as the revolution is televised—as the mutant birds Collins calls mockingjays know how to repeat a refrain, so the media can publicize symbolic actions in a way that may eventually bring down regimes.

"You have to fight on your own," the sadistic instructor tells the children in *Battle Royale*. "But that's how the game of life is anyway." To follow the plot of *Battle Royale*, it helps to make a list of the forty-two Japanese children and cross them off as they're eliminated—so you can double-check your tally; the number of students surviving is helpfully included at the end of each chapter. I've rarely seen my thirteen-year-old daughter as engrossed with books as she was both with *The Hunger Games* and with *Battle Royale*. And after reading the first chapter of *Battle Royale*, she was able to predict who the first few people to die would be quite accurately, having picked up on far more of the foreshadowing in that chapter than I did. This makes me wonder if the book shows a particular sensitivity to the social dynamics of middle school. Adolescence is when we notice the world is ruthlessly competitive, and that we are going to be forced to participate in it, when like Peeta in *The Hunger Games* we wish "to show the Capitol they don't own me. That I'm more than just a piece in their Games."

Having to kill people you don't know because your leaders tell you to has, since time immemorial, been most people's basic experience of war—indeed, this is something statistically even more likely to happen to people living in a tribal or aboriginal society than to those living under a totalitarian dictatorship. The body language of the teenagers in the movie version of *The Hunger Games* who, having tracked down a younger teenager who's made the mistake of building a camp fire, smile at her before killing her, is deeply disturbing because one instinctively recognizes an event that must have happened many times in humankind's long history.

Lord of the Flies

In [British author] William Golding's 1954 novel *Lord of the Flies*, a group of boys on an island revert to a "state of nature" in the absence of adult supervision. The book is set during, and is on some level about, World War Two, in which Golding served as a navàl officer—but despite the murderous nature of some key governments in that conflict, the point of *Lord of the Flies* is that the violence ultimately lies within us. Golding wrote of the ending of the novel, "The officer, having interrupted a man-hunt, prepares to take the children off the is-

Actors James Aubrey and Hugh Edwards play Ralph and Piggy, respectively, in the 1963 screen adaptation of William Golding's Lord of the Flies. © INTERFOTO/Cinema/Alamy.

land in a cruiser which will presently be hunting its enemy in the same implacable way. And who will rescue the adult and his cruiser?"

Neither *The Hunger Games* nor *Battle Royale* bother with the ominous landscape descriptions Golding gives us in *Lord of the Flies*, partly because for Takami and Collins the evil is not in our nature, but in our government. For the same reason, few of the contestants in these books succumb to delirium as the boys in *Lord of the Flies* do—with only a few exceptions; they handle their predicament as rationally as if they were competing in a video game. One sense in which *Lord of the Flies* may be the darkest of these books, despite its comparatively modest death toll—only two, murders—is that so many of its characters go mad. Even Ralph, the most clear-headed survivor in *Lord of the Flies*, keeps forgetting the boys' long-term goal is to be rescued rather than to thrive as sav-ges, and by the end all the other boys are united in trying to kill Ralph—whereas Katniss in *The Hunger Games* and Shuya in *Battle Royale* succeed against the odds in maintaining healthy alliances and remaining focused on a strategy, and only a few minor characters in those worlds go insane.

Moreover when a character in *Battle Royale* behaves evilly, Takami always supplies an explanation—this boy was born a sociopath, this girl was abused, most of the kids are just scared to trust each other in case they're taken advantage of—evil is not seen as humanity's default setting as it is in *Lord of the Flies*. *The Hunger Games* is less explicit on this ethical question, but the guiding principle of the series seems to be that people are good until power corrupts them. Both Takami and Collins portray the adult world as one of brutal conflict whose rules frustrate our normal instinct to cooperate. For Ralph, after he's been hunted, wildness loses its attraction, but Katniss draws power from nature—hunting in the woods is how she becomes resourceful enough to stand up to authority, and it's significant that even the harmful creatures she encounters there are not naturally occurring species, but mutations artificially engineered by her government.

While the government in *The Hunger Games* is staging a contest to punish the people for a past rebellion, the annual slaughter in *Battle Royale* is allegedly for military research purposes. Shogo in *Battle Royale* reflects our contemporary skepticism about government with the observation, "My guess is that when this lovely game was first proposed—some crazy military strategist probably came up with it—there was no opposition. You don't want to stir things up by questioning the specialists. And it's terribly difficult to end something that's already been established. You interfere, and you're out of a job."

How Fears Have Changed

A Robert Sheckley [American author] story from 1953 suggests how our fears have changed since that time. In "Seventh

Victim," the government determines that the only way to prevent war from destroying humanity is to provide alternative
outlets for men's urge to kill each other. Government-created
Emotional Catharsis Boards legalize murder for those who
want it. Many men and a few women sign up and are as-
signed a victim to kill—in return, they have to be a victim for
someone else, who they are permitted to kill in self-defense if
they are quick enough. Sheckley here treats murder as a natural human need that the government must, in the general interest, find a way to channel and control—an explanation that
today seems unimaginable even as satire.

At the close of the Korean War, it came naturally to Sheckley and Golding to portray people as the problem and government as the solution—Takami and Collins, writing in our
times, begin with the reverse assumption, and to make this
comparison is to sense how far, in the intervening decades, the
pendulum of consensus has swung from [Thomas] Hobbes
[who saw humans' natural state as evil] towards [Jean-Jacques]
Rousseau [who believed in the innocence of humankind].
Books like *Battle Royale* and *The Hunger Games* would have
seemed too subversive of adult authority to have been published or perhaps even conceived in the 1950s—but does this
mean we have become less naïve, or just that we have become
naïve in a different way?

The Mockingjay Revolution
Is Not a Just War

Louis Melançon

Louis Melançon holds master's degrees from the Joint Military Intelligence College in Washington, DC, and King's College in London and has been awarded the bronze star. He is a US Army officer.

Melançon investigates the Mockingjay rebellion through the lens of the "just war" tradition. The rebels may have sufficient cause to fight against the harsh ways of the Capitol, but when it comes to actual combat, they prove to be as ruthless as their opponents. In particular, when they target children and first responders toward the end of Mockingjay, *President Coin's forces violate the concept of* jus in bello, *or proper conduct in war. Melançon therefore cannot ultimately term the Mockingjay rebellion a just war. Though Panem does "stumble" upon peace in the epilogue to* Mockingjay, *Melançon considers this happy ending to be more a matter of luck than design.*

Panem is no stranger to violence: Children are murdered in the arena, and the rebellion unleashes devastation and destruction from the districts to the streets of the Capitol. Inside and outside the arena, Panem is a world at war. *The Hunger Games* trilogy is largely about the horrific costs of war: Innocent people (like Prim) are killed or maimed, and other basically good people (like Beetee and Gale) are driven to commit appalling acts of violence that they would never have contemplated in their civilian lives. In the aftermath of war, the survi-

Louis Melançon, "Starting Fires Can Get You Burned," in *The Hunger Games and Philosophy: A Critique of Pure Treason,* ed. George A. Dunn and Nicolas Michaud. John Wiley & Sons: 2012, pp. 222–234. Reproduced with permission of Wiley in the format Book via Copyright Clearance Center.

vors face not only horrendous physical devastation but also psychic wounds that may never heal and resentments that may never cease to fester.

Philosophers who have reflected on these costs have identified two crucial questions to ask about the morality of war. First, when, if ever, is the violence of war an acceptable way to settle differences? Second, if war *is* sometimes acceptable, are there any limits to what we may do to achieve our wartime objectives? Three different answers have been proposed to the question of the morality of war:

- No, violence against others is always unacceptable (*pacifism*).
- Sure, anything goes as long as the violence serves our side's needs (*political realism*).
- Maybe, but only if we have a just cause and only if we conduct the war in a just manner (*the just-war tradition*).

The just-war tradition is an ethical framework that has evolved over the centuries as a way to set limits on both when we may go to war and what we may do to win. Let's look at those proposed limits, using the Mockingjay revolution as a test case. Was it fought for the right reasons and in the right way? As much as we admire the plucky rebels inspired by Katniss Everdeen, we need to prepare ourselves for the possibility that the just-war tradition may not give an unqualified endorsement of every aspect of their conduct.

Stepping into the Arena

The military theorist Carl von Clausewitz (1780–1831) famously defined war as "a continuation of politics by other means." His point was that nations don't go to war because politicians and generals love violence for its own sake; rather, war is a tool used to achieve political goals that can't be achieved through nonviolent means. But can the use of such a destructive tool ever be moral?

Pacifism holds that the use of any violence is immoral, although exceptions are sometimes made for self-defense or the defense of innocent victims. Without those exceptions, though, a pacifist in Panem would last about as long as a juicy steak in front of a wolf mutation. Worse still, according to critics, the pacifist effectively yields the field to violent aggressors who don't share his or her scruples. The appeal of pacifism lies in its acknowledgment that war is a great evil, to be avoided as much as possible. But there are other evils in the world, such as political oppression, that we may be able to remedy through wholly nonviolent means.

Even though we don't find many pacifists in Panem, it seems like you can't let loose an arrow from your bow without it hitting a political realist. Presidents Snow and Coin are prime examples. For them, war really is just a tool, neither moral nor immoral. All that matters is whether a resort to violence furthers their interests—and that trumps every other consideration based on ideology, morality, or social norms. This point of view was summed up memorably in the account given by the ancient historian Thucydides (460–395 BCE) of how the city of Athens justified its brutal conquest of the island of Melos in 416 BCE: "The strong do what they have the power to do, the weak accept what they have to accept."

There could hardly be a better description of how the Capitol deals with the districts, controlling almost every aspect of their citizens' lives in order to maintain the Capitol's strength and keep the districts weak. The leadership of District 13, in contrast, lacks all of the military options of the Capitol and must pursue its objectives through more devious means, infiltrating the Capitol to create a network of spies and saboteurs to bring down President Snow and his regime. To the realist, neither group is either right or wrong; both are just doing "what they have the power to do" in order to advance their interests.

The great strength of political realism lies in its willingness to toss sentimentality aside and turn an unflinching eye on how the world actually works much of the time. The great drawback of political realism is that it doesn't hold out much hope of progress. If we wish to move to a point where war is no longer necessary to settle our differences, realism can offer us no guidance on how to get there. The just-war tradition, on the other hand, tries to take us down that road while recognizing that we're not yet at the point where nations can afford to adopt an official policy of pacifism.

What we know today as the just-war tradition dates back to the Roman Empire in the first century BCE and owes a great deal to contributions from both pagan philosophers, like Marcus Tullius Cicero (106–43 BCE), and Christian theologians, like Augustine of Hippo (354–430) and Thomas Aquinas (1225–1274). As it stands today, the tradition offers a set of norms that are generally accepted within the society of nation-states. It consists of three elements—the first two well established over the centuries and a third one that has emerged much more recently. They are *jus ad bellum* (the right to go to war), *jus in bello* (right conduct within war), and *jus post bellum* (justice after war). Each contains a set of criteria that must be satisfied in order for a war to be deemed just. If you can't meet every one of these criteria, then the just-war tradition says that you had better stay out of the arena.

As with pacifism and political realism, the just-war tradition has certain strengths and weaknesses. For our purposes, the Mockingjay revolution offers an excellent case study to highlight some of the virtues and potential pitfalls of the tradition.

Designing the Arena

In the just-war tradition, there are seven distinct criteria of *jus ad bellum* used to determine whether it's just to wage a war:

- *Just cause.* A war can be fought only to defend against a serious evil or to remedy a grave injustice, such as unprovoked aggression or a violation of basic human rights.

- *Right intention.* The goal of the war cannot be material gain; its sole purpose must be to achieve the just cause.

- *Last resort.* Every route to a peaceful resolution to the conflict must have been tried before going to war.

- *Probability for success.* It's wrong to start a war with no chance of success or one that can succeed only by resorting to methods that would be unjust because they violate the criteria of *jus in bello* (which we'll look at shortly).

- *Comparative justice.* It's rare that either party to a conflict has entirely clean hands or that one side is completely right while the other is completely wrong. Most often, both sides are guilty of some wrongdoing, although their misdeeds may not be of equal gravity. In order for a nation to justly declare war, its past conduct doesn't have to be utterly above reproach, but it must be significantly more in the right than its adversary is.

- *Proportionality.* The benefits of achieving the goals of the war must outweigh the death and destruction that will occur as a result.

- *Competent authority.* War can be declared only by a legitimate political authority, not by private individuals or groups.

The districts clearly seem to meet most of these criteria when they rebel against the Capitol. Violation of basic human rights is all in a day's work for the Capitol, so the districts have *just cause* for their rebellion. And as long as the real aim of the rebellion is to establish a just regime, the rebels are fighting with the *right intention*. (We'll leave aside for now President Coin's plan to install herself as a new tyrant.) Any peaceful overtures to bring about change would be met with the violence of Snow's peacekeepers—who are obviously operating with a different definition of the word *peace*—so the rebels turn to armed struggle only as a *last resort*.

Moreover, the Dark Days showed that it's possible to overcome the military power of the Capitol, so the rebels have sufficient *probability for success*. Ending the abuses of the Capitol and establishing justice would bring tremendous improvement to the lives of the people in the districts, a goal that is arguably worth the cost in death and destruction. So the criterion of *proportionality* may also be met.

Two criteria, though, leap out as potential problems for the rebels: *comparative justice* and *competent authority*.

Some philosophers have wanted to eliminate comparative justice as a criterion because of the way militaristic regimes like the Capitol can twist it around to justify their acts of aggression and oppression. After all, the Capitol might insist that it suffered horrible injustices during the turmoil of the Dark Days and so now has the right to keep the districts permanently under its heel to prevent those days from recurring.

"Oh, come on!" you're probably thinking. "Just look at how the Capitol treats the districts. Isn't the sacrifice of two children a year for the Capitol's entertainment an injustice that far outweighs whatever the Capitol may have suffered during the Dark Days?" If you ask me, it certainly is! But critics of the comparative justice criterion argue that weighing one wrong against another can sometimes be like comparing burned bread to tracker jackers—they may just be too dissimilar for any meaningful comparison. In any case, let's set these concerns aside and grant that the Mockingjay revolution can probably fulfill this criterion, even if the criterion itself has some problems.

Justice Doesn't Require a "Justice Building"

The criterion of competent authority is a bigger stumbling block for the Mockingjay revolution—and, as we'll see, for the just-war tradition as a whole—since it has traditionally been thought that legitimate political authority requires a state: a nation of people under a government that's recognized by other governments. Only such a legitimate state authority can authorize the waging of war. For Panem's Capitol and District 13, this criterion poses no problem. Whatever political arrangements may exist elsewhere in this future world, North America includes these two states. District 13 can therefore claim competent authority to wage war against the Capitol, and vice versa.

But whereas District 13 provides sanctuary, training, weapons, and some armed forces for the rebellion, it's the other districts that are really doing the fighting. If they must meet the criterion of competent authority before they can rebel against the Capitol, they're out of luck, because the rebel leadership in the various districts is not a legitimate state.

So it looks like the Capitol can claim that it's simply defending itself against an unjust band of lawbreakers—terrorist hooligans!—whose violence isn't sanctioned by any legitimate authority. Does the just-war tradition really leave the people of the districts high and dry, denying them any right to revolution? If we interpret the criterion of competent authority in a strict and literal sense, then I'm afraid so. This inability of the just-war tradition to permit an otherwise wholly justified use of organized violence looks like a significant weakness of *jus ad bellum*.

There are other ways we could interpret this criterion, however. We could, for example, define *legitimate authority* as any expression of popular self-determination, chucking the requirement that some state authority must ratify it. However, deciding what counts as a valid expression of popular self-determination can be just as tough as applying the criterion of comparative justice. For one thing, there's always a risk that elements with less than honorable intentions might mask their true goals behind a claim to be fighting for the people.

President Coin is a flagrant example of this sort of duplicity. She spurs on the rebellion, stoking the aspirations of the districts to break free from the Capitol's oppressive grip, but her real goal is only to increase her own power and secure the resources of Panem for herself, not to correct the Capitol's injustices.

In any case, if we regard legitimacy as something that originates with the people rather than with government authority, then the actions of the rebels in the Mockingjay revolution might be permitted within the just-war tradition. Without this definition of legitimacy, however, it's not a just conflict. That's not to say the districts shouldn't have rebelled. What we learn from examples like the Mockingjay revolution is that *jus ad bellum* must be updated. Otherwise, uprisings by even the most horribly oppressed peoples are unjust, and downtrodden populations all over the world should simply stop fighting for their freedom.

Cracking the Nut

Regardless of whether the districts fulfilled all of the criteria of *jus ad bellum* before they launched their rebellion, once the spark ignited, violence engulfed the districts like wildfire. Is there any way to contain such violence in a time of war? For an answer to that question, let's consider *jus in bello*. *Jus in bello* is more focused than *jus ad bellum*, and that focus is on actual combat.

The first criterion, the *principle of distinction*, requires military operations to distinguish between combatant—actual soldiers engaged in combat or providing logistical support— and civilian noncombatants. Enemy soldiers are fair game, but the direct targeting of noncombatants (through, for instance, bombing a residential neighborhood) is strictly prohibited. *Jus in bello* criteria generally focus on offensive actions, but it could be argued that it's equally wrong for the military to endanger its own civilians by setting up a military base next to a school or a hospital or by using civilians as human shields.

The second criterion is the *principle of military necessity.* Given the destructiveness of war, the military must use only the minimum amount of force necessary to achieve its objectives.

The third criterion is the *principle of proportionality.* Even if civilians aren't directly targeted and force is kept to a bare minimum, military actions might still result in the deaths of noncombatants as a foreseen but unintended consequence—"collateral damage," as it's often euphemistically called. The *jus in bello* principle of proportionality differs from *jus ad bellum*'s proportionality, which requires that enough anticipated benefit come out of the war as a whole to offset all of the death and destruction. Here the principle focuses on particular military actions, insisting that the military benefit derived from an assault outweigh any resulting noncombatant deaths.

Unfortunately for the noncombatants, both sides in the Mockingjay revolution violate these criteria. Let's face it; no one expects the Capitol to put forth a lot of effort trying to wage a just war. However, the Capitol not only neglects the principle of distinction, it also appears to be actively committed to flouting it! Granted, it can be difficult to distinguish between military targets and the general population in a revolution, an insurgency, or a civil war, but this distinction doesn't even seem to matter to the Capitol when it undertakes its blanket reprisals, targeting makeshift hospitals and firebombing entire districts out of existence.

Of course, the Capitol's disregard of the principle of distinction doesn't grant the rebels or District 13 a free pass to do the same. Nor are they allowed to ignore any of the other criteria of *jus in bello* just because their enemy has shown so little respect for human life. Unfortunately for the people of Panem, no one seems to have gotten that memo.

The principle of distinction is breached on both sides in the final push against President Snow's residence, when a living obstacle of children is placed between the attacking rebel forces and their target. The use of children—or any other noncombatants—as shields to induce the other party to violate *jus in bello* is beyond the pale, but the actions that resolved the situation are no less foul. Bombing the children and then setting booby traps for the medical personnel trying to save them is a flagrant and despicable violation of the principle of distinction, regardless of whether this was the work of the Capitol or District 13.

There may be some doubt about who was responsible, but let's trust the gut instincts of our heroine, who tells us that President Coin and her war council bear the guilt. If so, then they threw the principle of distinction out the window twice, first by directly targeting the human shields and then by targeting the first responders, who are traditionally granted noncombatant status on the battlefield even when they're in uniform. With that act, the rebellion proved to be as bad as the Capitol and forfeited any claim to *jus in bello*.

The rebels, though, had already lost their moral halo sometime earlier. In the siege of the Nut, they violated the principles of military necessity and proportionality. By that stage of the war, District 2 and the Capitol were isolated, but the rest of Panem was more or less liberated and independent of Capitol control. Even large portions of District 2 were in rebel hands, and the once feared Capitol airpower was no longer a threat. The only remaining Capitol strongholds in District 2 were the Nut—a mine-turned-fortress complex—and some neighborhoods of the adjacent city. Besieged peacekeepers holed up in the Nut could repel rebel attacks, but they couldn't mount an effective counterattack to drive the rebels from District 2 and relieve the pressure on the Capitol.

From the perspective of *jus in bello*, then, the question the rebels should have asked themselves was this: Does the Nut have to be attacked at all to achieve the goal of independence from the Capitol? The answer is no. Ending the siege at that point was not a military necessity. To continue their final drive against President Snow, the rebels needed only to keep the peacekeepers within the Nut on the defensive by deploying minimal force to maintain the siege. Instead, they set off an avalanche to end the siege, unnecessarily killing large numbers of both peacekeepers and District 2 civilians trapped within the Nut, thereby also violating the principle of proportionality. So even before the tragedy in the Capitol, the rebels had forfeited their *jus in bello* medallion.

Putting Out the Fire

Once a war has realized its (ideally) just aims through (ideally) just means, we need to stop the fighting—but even in peace the just-war tradition still has much guidance to offer. The conclusion and the aftermath of wartime hostilities also have to be handled in a just manner. Otherwise, we only create new grievances and plant the seeds for the next war, as the Capitol did at the end of the Dark Days by imposing draconian punishments like the Hunger Games. A new element of the just-war tradition, *jus post bellum*, addresses this issue.

According to *jus post bellum*, before we even embark on a war, we need to formulate our vision of what the world should look like when the war is over: What conditions will have to be met before we can declare an end to hostilities? How can we rehabilitate, reconstruct, and reform the unjust institutions that led to war, and thus secure a lasting peace? What resources will we need to commit to that task? *Jus post bellum* also prohibits extraordinary punitive measures, such as the Hunger Games, and requires that we punish all war criminals, regardless of which side they were on. The goal is to create a just post-conflict situation that won't give rise to resentments that could easily lead to a future war.

To its credit, the rebel leadership in Panem does have a rough vision for the aftermath of the war: Snow must be out and there must be no more centralized control from the Capitol. The details get a bit fuzzy after that, though. Coin wants some of the centralized control passed to her, whereas others want the new Panem to adhere to a more republican model.

But it's the punitive measures contemplated by the rebels—specifically, a final Hunger Games with only the Capitol's children as tributes—that most seriously run afoul of *jus post bellum*. Had they actually implemented that proposal, they would have been guilty of the same injustice perpetrated by the Capitol. Fortunately, the new regime abandons the plan to kill innocent Capitol children. Even so, there appears to be little appetite to address war crimes committed within the rebel ranks, such as the firebomb that targeted noncombatants, whereas criminals like President Snow get speedy trials and swiftly executed justice.

The *Mockingjay* epilogue suggests that the people of Panem may be heading toward that ever elusive desideratum [something needed] known as a peaceful future. If they're successful, however, it's because they have merely stumbled into success. The Mockingjay revolution, it turns out, was not a just war. Technically, not acting on behalf of a legitimate state prevents the rebels from fulfilling the requirement that war be declared by a competent authority—unless, of course, we adopt a more flexible definition of political authority.

That's hardly their most serious infraction, though, from the perspective of the just-war tradition. The rebels' actions in the course of the war make them no better than the Capitol, and their behavior at the conclusion of the fighting does little to move Panem toward a more peaceful tomorrow. To find peace despite all of these stumbles would be quite a stroke of luck.

Unfortunately, our world doesn't seem to have the same measure of luck working in its favor. Instead, we have more ongoing conflicts and potential conflicts than anyone can count, many the products of long-standing grievances constantly bubbling up from the past. From the vantage point of our own exceedingly bloody moment in history, it seems like a pipe dream to imagine that organized human violence could ever be completely eradicated.

The just-war tradition does not promise such eradication, however. Instead, it promises to help us rein in some of the destructiveness of war while pushing us to seek a more peaceful future. Most important, the just-war tradition helps to ensure that real-world conflicts, unlike the Mockingjay revolution, don't just stumble into peace but actively seek it instead.

Contemporary
Perspectives on Violence

Violent Teens Should Not Be Treated as Adults

Sarah Alice Brown

Sarah Alice Brown covers juvenile justice issues for the National Conference of State Legislatures.

In the following viewpoint, Brown writes that many lawmakers are reconsidering how they deal with violent youthful offenders. Two major developments have factored into the new thinking: Youth crime has decreased dramatically in recent years, and current research indicates that the teenage brain is not fully developed. Studies show that the human brain may not become fully adult until a person reaches twenty-five years of age. Many youths react impulsively to situations that they might otherwise be able to handle if they were older. In fact, Brown writes, many violent youths do not grow up to be violent adults; instead, they mature as they grow older. Lawmakers in many states have rewritten laws and altered policy to reflect this new understanding that teens are not adults and should not be treated the same under the law.

Juvenile justice policy is at a crossroads. Juvenile crime has decreased. Recent brain and behavioral science research has revealed new insights into how and when adolescents develop. And state budgets remain tight. Together, these factors have led many lawmakers to focus on which approaches can save money, yet keep the public safe and treat young offenders more effectively.

Why Now?

When youth violence reached a peak more than 20 years ago, the country lost confidence in its ability to rehabilitate juve-

Sarah Alice Brown, "Kids Are Not Adults: Brain Research Is Providing New Insights into What Drives Teenage Behavior, Moving Lawmakers to Rethink Policies That Treat Them Like Adults," *State Legislatures*, vol. 39, no. 4, 2013. Copyright © 2013 by the National Conference of State Legislatures. All rights reserved. Reproduced by permission.

niles. Legislatures responded by passing laws allowing more young offenders to be tried as adults. Since then, however, juvenile crime has steadily declined.

Between 1994 and 2010, violent crime arrest rates decreased for all age groups, but more for juveniles than for adults. More specifically, the rates dropped an average of 54 percent for teenagers 15 to 17, compared to 38 percent for those between 18 and 39. And while arrest rates for violent crimes were higher in 2010 than in 1980 for all ages over 24, the rates for juveniles ages 15 to 17 were down from 1980.

With the steady decline in juvenile violence, the current state of the economy and new information on how brain development shapes teens' behavior, some lawmakers are reconsidering past assumptions.

Legislatures across the country are working on their juvenile justice policies, from passing individual measures to revamping entire codes. Arkansas revised its juvenile justice code in 2009; Georgia and Kentucky are considering doing so, and many other states are at various stages of making changes in juvenile justice.

"It's time to bring the juvenile code back to current times and find methods that work by looking at best practices nationally," says Georgia Representative Wendell Willard (R), who introduced a bill to revise the code this session [2013]. "We need to incorporate key items, such as instruments to assess risks, and put interventions in place within communities for young people involved in the system," says Willard.

Last year, lawmakers in Kentucky formed a task force to study juvenile justice issues. The group will recommend whether to amend any of the state's current juvenile code in 2013. "Frankly, our juvenile code is out of date, but this task force will give the legislature the foundation to change that and reflect best practices nationwide," says Representative John Tilley (D), co-chair of the task force.

Changes are not always easily made, and states are at different stages of reform. Among the various viewpoints and depths of changes, however, is the generally agreed-upon belief that juveniles are different from adults.

For Adults Only

Research distinguishing adolescents from adults has led states to reestablish boundaries between the criminal and juvenile justice systems. New policies reflect the growing body of research on how the brain develops, which has discovered teens' brains do not fully develop until about age 25, according to the John D. and Catherine T. MacArthur Foundation's Research Network on Adolescent Development and Juvenile Justice. Other social science and behavioral science also shows that kids focus on short-term payoffs rather than long-term consequences of their actions and engage in immature, emotional, risky, aggressive and impulsive behavior and delinquent acts.

Dr. David Fassler, a psychiatry professor at the University of Vermont College of Medicine, has testified before legislative committees on brain development. He says the research helps explain—not excuse—teenage behavior.

"It doesn't mean adolescents can't make rational decisions or appreciate the difference between right and wrong. But it does mean that, particularly when confronted with stressful or emotional circumstances, they are more likely to act impulsively, on instinct, without fully understanding or considering the consequences of their actions."

"Every single adult has been a teenager, and many have also raised them. We all know firsthand the mistakes teens can make simply without thinking. Now we have the science that backs this up," says North Carolina Representative Marilyn Avila (R). She is working to increase the age at which teenagers can be tried as adults from 16 to 18 in her state.

Other states are considering similar changes. Lawmakers in Colorado passed significant changes in 2012, barring district attorneys from charging juveniles as adults for many low- and mid-level felonies. For serious crimes, they raised the age at which offenders can be tried as adults from 14 to 16.

In Nevada, Mississippi and Utah, lawmakers now leave it up to the juvenile courts to decide whether to transfer a juvenile to adult court. The Oklahoma legislature upped the age limit at which offenders can be tried as adults for misdemeanors to 18 and one-half. And Ohio now requires a judicial review before transferring anyone under age 21 to an adult jail.

Counsel Is Key

A related trend in the past decade is to increase due process protections to preserve the constitutional rights of young offenders to ensure that youths understand the court process, make reasonable decisions regarding their case and have adequate counsel. At least 10 states now have laws requiring qualified counsel to accompany juveniles at various stages of youth court proceedings. For juveniles appealing their cases, Utah created an expedited process. And two new laws in Pennsylvania require that all juvenile defendants be represented by counsel and that juvenile court judges state in court the reasoning behind their sentences.

To protect the constitutional rights of young offenders, Massachusetts Senator Karen Spilka (D) says "it is important for states to ensure that juveniles have access to quality counsel." The Bay State created juvenile defense resource centers that provide leadership, training and support to the entire Massachusetts juvenile defense bar.

Legislators are also enacting laws on determining the competency of juvenile offenders to stand trial. At least 16 states— Arizona, California, Colorado, Delaware, Florida, Georgia, Idaho, Kansas, Louisiana, Maine, Michigan, Minnesota, Nebraska, Ohio, Texas and Virginia—and the District of Columbia, now specifically address competency in statute. For example, Idaho lawmakers established standards for evaluating a juvenile's competency to proceed. Maine passed a similar measure that defines "chronological immaturity," "mental illness" and "mental retardation" for use in determining juvenile competency.

Between 65 percent and 70 percent of the 2 million young people arrested each year in the United States have some type of mental health disorder. Newer policies focus on providing more effective evaluations and interventions for youths who come into contact with the juvenile justice system. This includes proper screening, assessment and treatment services for young offenders. Some states have special mental health courts to provide intensive case management as well.

New mental health assessments in Louisiana and Pennsylvania give a wide range of professionals the means to reliably ascertain youths' needs. And other states such as Colorado, Connecticut, Ohio and Texas have passed comprehensive juvenile mental health reform laws.

Family Matters

"Show me it will work, and then I am all for it!" says North Carolina's Avila. "As a legislator, I am very much in favor of evidence-based programming, because I want to invest in what will work." She cites the effectiveness of three kinds of programs that have passed the evaluation test and are being used in at least 10 states. They include the families in the treatments young offenders receive to address specific behaviors to improve positive results for the whole family.

• Multi-systemic therapy teaches parents how to effectively handle the high-risk "acting out" behaviors of teenagers.

• Family functional therapy focuses on teaching communication and problem-solving skills to the whole family.

• Aggression-replacement training teaches positive ways to express anger as well as anger control and moral reasoning.

Massachusetts Senator Spilka believes these kinds of programs are important because "instead of simply focusing on the child's behavior, they look to effectively treat and help the entire family."

Communities Are Key

Policy makers across the country are searching for ways to keep the public safe while reducing costs. Many are looking at effective policies that divert young offenders away from expensive, secure correctional facilities and into local community programs. According to the U.S. Office of Juvenile Justice and Delinquency Prevention, incarceration is a costly and ineffective way to keep delinquent juveniles from committing more serious crimes. Researchers suggest, instead, in investing in successful and cost-effective programs that have undergone rigorous evaluations.

For example, RECLAIM Ohio is a national model for funding reform that channels the money saved from fewer juvenile commitments into local courts to be used in treating and rehabilitating young people. The program not only has reduced juvenile commitments to detention facilities and saved money, but also has cut down on the number of young people re-entering the justice system. The cost of housing 10 young people in a Department of Youth Services' facility is $571,940 a year versus $85,390 a year for the RECLAIM Ohio program.

Realignment shifts responsibility for managing young offenders from states to the counties. Such strategies are based on the premise that local communities are in the best position to provide extensive and cost-effective supervision and treatment services for juvenile offenders, and that youth are more successful when supervised and treated closer to their homes and families.

Illinois lawmakers, for example, passed major changes in 2004 that created Redeploy Illinois, which encourages counties to develop community programs for juveniles rather than confine them in state correctional facilities.

The program gives counties financial support to provide comprehensive services in their home communities to delinquent youths who might otherwise be sent to the Illinois Department of Juvenile Justice. The program has been so successful that it is expanding statewide and has become a model for other states.

Several other states, from California and Georgia, to New York and Texas, are also looking at ways to effectively and safely redirect fiscal resources from state institutions to community services.

"Getting kids out of the correctional centers and treated in the community is obviously the best practice," says Georgia's Willard. "You have to close these large infrastructures and the overhead that goes with it, so you can redirect that money to treating youth in the community. When you go about such an exercise in your own communities, you will accomplish the goal of saving money."

States also are shortening the time juveniles are confined in detention centers, usually while they wait for a court appearance or disposition. A recent Mississippi law, for example, limits it to 10 days for first-time nonviolent youth offenders. And Georgia decreased it from 60 days to 30 days. Illinois lawmakers increased the age of kids who can be detained for more than six hours in a county jail or municipal lockup from age 12 to 17.

Young Offenders Grow Up

Violence toward others tends to peak in adolescence, beginning most often around age 16, according to Emory University psychiatrist Peter Ash. However, if a teenager hasn't committed a violent crime by age 19, he's unlikely to become violent later, Ash says. The promising news is that 66 percent to 75 percent of violent young people grow out of it. "They get more self-controlled."

Realizing that teens who commit delinquent acts don't always turn into adult criminals, more states are protecting the confidentiality of juvenile records for future educational and employment opportunities to help them make successful transitions into adulthood.

In 2011, Delaware lawmakers passed legislation allowing juvenile criminal cases that are dismissed, acquitted or not prosecuted to be expunged from a young person's record. "Children who are charged with minor crimes that are dismissed or dropped should not have these charges following them around for the rest of their lives," says Representative Michael A. Barbieri (D), sponsor of the bill.

And in 2012, eight states—California, Colorado, Hawaii, Louisiana, Ohio, Oregon, Vermont and Washington—enacted laws vacating or expunging any prostitution charges juvenile victims of sex trafficking may have received.

A Bipartisan Issue

These recent legislative trends reflect a new understanding of adolescent development. Investing in alternative programs in the community instead of incarceration and adopting only proven intervention programs are among the examples of how state legislators hope to better serve youth and prevent juvenile crime.

"Reforming juvenile justice is definitely a bipartisan issue that all legislators can get behind. It is the right time. All the research says it makes sense and will save money," says Representative Avila from North Carolina.

There Is No Correlation Between Violent Movies and Societal Violence

Robert M. Schwartz

Robert M. Schwartz is a partner in the O'Melveny & Meyers law firm in Los Angeles, California, and has represented filmmakers, studios, and distributors in lawsuits claiming that movies cause crime.

In the following viewpoint, Schwartz contends that although the entertainment industry, particularly the motion picture business, is usually blamed whenever a mass murder occurs, there is no consensus among researchers that media violence causes such actions. He argues that "expressive" works have always been violent and that courts have ruled against plaintiffs who try to seek recompense from artists because the bar for a guilty verdict is justly set very high; victims of violence must prove that a film or other expressive work explicitly directs its audience to go forth and commit a violent crime. This is as it should be, Schwartz believes, and it is in harmony with the First Amendment, which protects the artist's right to create an imaginative work. Schwartz does admit that any national conversation about societal violence should involve the entertainment industry, but feels that blaming the industry or seeking to impose liability on filmmakers is not a solution to the problem of societal violence.

When an act of mass murder occurs, the entertainment industry is invariably put on a short list of potential culprits. Critics assert that movies and television programs depict violence excessively and insensitively, market the content inappropriately and are responsible for creating a culture of violence and inhumanity.

Expressive Works Have Always Been Violent

Some also ask whether the entertainment industry is culpable not only morally, but legally. The answer should be no. Usually, the courts or the legislative system are invoked in an attempt to impose liability on filmmakers and distributors for allegedly inspiring the perpetrators to commit their heinous acts. Alternatively, the legal system is asked to regulate the content—or at least the advertising—of motion pictures, television programs, video games and other expressive works. Having represented industry members in both areas, it's my opinion that our resources would be better spent looking elsewhere for solutions.

Those who say that Hollywood, particularly in the past 20 years, has created a culture of violence have forgotten that expressive works—ranging from Homer to the Bible, Shakespeare and Renaissance painters—have depicted violence in brutal detail for thousands of years. And long before Hollywood became a target for blame, motion pictures had for decades depicted inhumane violence in such films as *Birth of a Nation, Grand Illusion, On the Waterfront* and *Lawrence of Arabia.*

A High Bar for Liability

A threshold concern with using the legal system against content creators is that there is no consensus among social scientists as to the effect on individual behavior of viewing violent motion pictures or other expressive works. It is not asking too much to require a meaningful causal link between one and the other before legislation or legal liability are to be imposed.

Most importantly, there is the First Amendment. Our founders established more than 200 years ago that the government could pass no law restricting the freedom of speech. The

Supreme Court has from time to time given guidance on what that principle means, including when concerns arose that speakers had said things that could cause others to act violently. The rule of law that governs here, from the court's 1969 *Brandenburg v. Ohio* decision, is that a filmmaker can have liability for the violent acts of another only if the work intentionally incites imminent unlawful action and is likely to do so.

That is a very high bar to imposing liability, as it should be. As a practical matter, it means that unless the filmmaker or the content "tells" the audience to leave the theater and engage in violent action, the fact that a motion picture depicts violence, and the fact that some unhinged person later claims that the film "inspired" the crime, are not enough to impose liability on the filmmaker.

For that reason, cases such as the one filed against [director] Oliver Stone and the studio that produced *Natural Born Killers*, in which the family of a murder victim claimed that the perpetrators were "acting out" what they saw in the movie, were decided in favor of the defendants without having to impanel a jury. No matter what one thought of the depictions of violence in that film, it contained nothing close to an exhortation to the audience to imminently commit acts of violence. In fact, as in similar cases, years had transpired between the release of the motion picture and the criminal conduct.

Debating Marketing Restrictions

Aware that the First Amendment protects the content of a motion picture, Congress and state legislatures have reacted to these tragedies by asking whether restrictions should be placed on the marketing of, and access to, works that depict violence.

In 1999, following the shooting at Columbine High School [in Colorado], President Clinton directed the FTC [Federal Trade Commission] and the Dept. of Justice to study whether entertainment that depicts violence was being improperly marketed to children. The studios, record companies and video game publishers turned over marketing plans, media buys and other documents. The government issued a report and has conducted follow-up investigations every few years thereafter.

Despite calls to regulate how the industry marketed violent content, the government recognized that the voluntary system the industry imposed on itself, starting with the film ratings system, did its job. To make that process the subject of a government takeover would require the creation of a "Ministry of Culture" and the imposition of subjective criteria that inevitably would run headlong into the First Amendment.

None of this is to say that the entertainment industry should have no part in the national conversation about acts of violence that horrify us. But turning to the courts or Congress to impose liability on the industry for such acts is not a solution to this problem. The industry is fortunate that the Supreme Court has made that clear.

Media Violence and the Connecticut Shootings

James Hirsen

James Hirsen holds a law degree and a master's in media psychology. He is a New York Times *best-selling author, media analyst, and law professor.*

In the aftermath of mass killings in Aurora, Colorado, and Newtown, Connecticut, in late 2012, Hirsen declares that it is time to reassess how violent media affects those who are susceptible to its influence. Even some movie people, such as producer Harvey Weinstein and actor Jamie Foxx, have recognized that film violence is now a concern that can no longer be ignored. Similarly, violent video games can be shown to have an addictive quality that may lead to acting out aggressions in the real world. Hirsen concludes by suggesting that better and more universal rating systems are needed to assist parents in evaluating their children's media choices.

Following the shocking events that took place in [Newtown] Connecticut last week [in December 2012], it is important that a discussion ensue in which the increased occurrence of mass shootings is examined in relation to the violence present in various forms of the entertainment media.

In a recent Fox News appearance, [Connecticut] Sen. Joe Lieberman insisted that producers of violent movies and video games must be asked to "tone it down," characterizing violence in entertainment as "a causative factor" that may lead to tragic incidents such as the one that occurred in Newtown.

James Hirsen, "Media Violence and the Conn. Shootings," *Newsmax*, December 17, 2012. Copyright © 2012 by Newsmax Media, Inc. All rights reserved. Reproduced by permission.

Making reference to a "direct connection" between people who have some mental instability and digital gaming, Colorado Gov. John Hickenlooper, in an appearance on Sunday's CNN *State of the Union* program, said, "When they go over the edge—they transport themselves, they become part of one of those video games."

Hickenlooper's comments are particularly significant since earlier in the year a mass shooting took place at a movie theater in the governor's state in which 12 people were killed and 58 wounded.

In reaction to the horrific Colorado movie theater shooting, studio mogul Harvey Weinstein at the time called for an entertainment industry summit to take a serious look at cinema violence.

"Fortunately, I've made enough money from producing violent movies, that I'm in a position to say Hollywood needs to stop making them," Weinstein said.

Weinstein knows a great deal about violent content, having produced Quentin Tarantino movie fare that includes *Pulp Fiction, Kill Bill,* and *Inglourious Basterds.*

Unfortunately, just days after calling for the summit Weinstein announced plans to premiere Tarantino's extremely violent *Django Unchained* in an apparent move to generate Oscar buzz for one of his company's movies.

In the wake of the Connecticut shootings, Jamie Foxx, star of the blood-soaked *Django Unchained,* publicly criticized the film industry, stating that the entertainment business needs to take responsibility for the violence it puts forth.

"We cannot turn our back and say that violence in films or anything that we do doesn't have a sort of influence," Foxx said at a recent press event for his latest film. "It does."

Meanwhile, entertainment companies were quick to alter some of the plans and special events that had been scheduled.

Teenage couple plays a shooting game in a video arcade. Many experts speculate that violent video games can lead to violent actions in society. © PhotoAlto via AP Images.

Paramount Pictures postponed the new Tom Cruise action movie *Jack Reacher* and Fox pulled new episodes of *Family Guy* and *American Dad.*

The time has come for industry figures to take the lead in examining the violent content of entertainment products. Empirical data now exists that links violent content in a variety of media forms to overly aggressive behavior in individuals.

The video gaming industry, however, is of the most pressing concern and deserves particular scrutiny due to the unique characteristics inherent in video game products and the greater potentiality for negative societal consequences as a result of active engagement.

Video games are distinctively interactive and have actually been shown to have addictive qualities. Many of the games are laden with highly charged content.

In November 2012 an Australian National University psychology researcher confirmed the addictive nature of video games, discovering that frequent gamers had "attentional bias," i.e., individuals were unable to stop thinking about gaming when attempting to focus on other tasks, a phenomenon that also occurs in alcohol, drug, and gambling addictions.

When the video gaming addiction occurs during adolescence, other developmental issues may arise including difficulty in successfully acquiring the social skills necessary to establish and maintain healthy relationships. A social awkwardness and/or isolationism related to the gaming addiction may result, which may feed upon itself as the addicted individual retreats further into a digital world.

Technology such as 3-D and HD imagery has enabled video game production to escalate its graphic intensity. The violence has become disturbingly realistic, and games may include themes that encourage and even reward players who are "successful" in the virtual participation in torture, sadism, and gruesome brutality.

In December 2012 research published in the *Journal of Experimental Social Psychology* shed light on the long-term effects of playing violent video games. In the research study, an individual who played a violent video game for three consecutive days was found to exhibit escalations in aggressive behavior and hostile expectations.

Parents, of course, would be wise to equip themselves with as much information as possible about the video games in which their children are engaging and to which their children are being exposed in order to best protect them.

The Entertainment Software Rating Board, the nonprofit, self-regulatory body that assigns ratings for video games, is in need of revision so that the rankings are clear, precise, and more user-friendly for parents.

Additionally, rather than having separate rating systems for films, television, music, and video games, a uniform system that utilizes consistent criteria would assist parents in product evaluation and better serve the public.

Media Violence by Itself Does Not Cause Mass Killings

Arline Kaplan

Arline Kaplan writes for Psychiatric Times. *She is also a writer in the health and business fields.*

In the following viewpoint, Kaplan states that speculation about the mass shooting at a showing of The Dark Knight Rises *in 2012 has rekindled the debate over whether media violence can be directly linked to violent crime. Media violence is everywhere today and functions as what one psychiatrist calls propaganda. The entertainment industry essentially provides advertisements for guns every time it shows a violent scene. While not all researchers agree that media violence is directly linked to crime, a number of recent studies suggest that continued exposure to screen violence alters the brain in undesirable ways. Nevertheless, Kaplan concludes, most viewers do not act on violent impulses unless there are other contributing factors; media violence is only one of several factors in predicting aggression.*

Speculation as to the causes of the recent mass shooting at a Batman movie screening in Colorado [in July 2012] has reignited debates in the psychiatric community about media violence and its effects on human behavior.

Ubiquitous Violence Propaganda

"Violence in the media has been increasing and reaching proportions that are dangerous," said Emanuel Tanay, MD, a retired clinical professor of psychiatry at Wayne State University and a forensic psychiatrist for more than 50 years.

"You turn on the television, and violence is there. You go to a movie, and violence is there," Tanay told *Psychiatric Times.* "Reality is distorted. If you live in a fictional world, then the fictional world becomes your reality."

The average American watches nearly 5 hours of video each day, 98% of which is watched on a traditional television set, according to Nielsen Company. Nearly two-thirds of TV programs contain some physical violence. Most self-involving video games contain some violent content, even those for children.

Tanay noted, "Anything that promotes something can be called propaganda. What we call entertainment is really propaganda for violence. If you manufacture guns, you don't need to advertise, because it is done by our entertainment industry."

In reality, the number of violent crimes has been falling, but the public's perception is that violence has increased. According to the US Bureau of Justice Statistics, the overall violent victimization rate (e.g., rape and assaults) decreased by 40% from 2001 to 2010. Similarly, the murder rate in the United States has dropped by almost half, from 9.8 per 100,000 people in 1991 to 5.0 in 2009.

Yet the propaganda, Tanay said, makes people feel that crime is everywhere and that guns are needed for protection.

Asked about the hundreds of murderers he has examined and possible links to media violence, Tanay said, "Most homicides are committed by people who know each other, and who have some momentary conflict and have a weapon handy. Usually only hit men, who are very rare, kill strangers."

Tanay did acknowledge, however, that some mentally ill individuals are vulnerable to dramatized violence. "They are naturally more vulnerable, because they are in the community, they are sick, and they may misinterpret something."

The 2 teenage boys who murdered 12 schoolmates and a teacher and injured 21 others at Columbine High School in

Invited guests make their way into a reopening ceremony and evening of remembrance at the Cinemark Century 16 Theaters on January 17, 2013, in Aurora, Colorado. The theater was the site of a mass shooting on July 20, 2012, that killed twelve people and wounded dozens of others. © Marc Piscotty/Getty Images News/Getty Images.

Colorado before killing themselves, he said, lived in a pathological environment. "Their lives centered around violent video games."

After the 1999 Columbine tragedy, the FBI [Federal Bureau of Investigation] and its team of psychiatrists and psychologists concluded that both perpetrators were mentally ill—Eric Harris was a psychopath and Dylan Klebold was depressive and suicidal. Other analysts have argued that a possible causal factor may relate to the young killers' obsessions with violent imagery in video games and movies that led them to depersonalize their victims.

While the vast majority of individuals afflicted with a psychotic disorder do not commit violence, Tanay said, "some mass killings have been perpetrated by people who are psychotic."

He cited the example of Seung-Hui Cho, a student who in 2007 shot to death 32 students and faculty of Virginia Tech, wounded 17 more, and then killed himself. "Cho was psychotic. Twenty years ago he would have been committed to a state hospital. . . . Now, we don't take care of psychotic patients until they do something violent," Tanay said.

Writing about the Colorado tragedy in a July 20 *Time* magazine essay, Christopher Ferguson, PhD, interim chair and associate professor of Psychology, Department of Psychology and Communication at Texas A&M International University, argued there is currently no scientific proof that the mass homicides can be explained, even in part, by violent entertainment.

Research Studies

So what does research show?

A 2002 report by the US Secret Service and the US Department of Education, which examined 37 incidents of targeted school shootings and school attacks from 1974 to 2000 in this country, found that "over half of the attackers demonstrated some interest in violence through movies, video games, books, and other media."

In a 2009 Policy Statement on Media Violence, the American Academy of Pediatrics said, "Extensive research evidence indicates that media violence can contribute to aggressive behavior, desensitization to violence, nightmares, and fear of being harmed."

This year, the Media Violence Commission of the International Society for Research on Aggression (ISRA) in its report on media violence said, "Over the past 50 years, a large number of studies conducted around the world have shown that watching violent television, watching violent films, or playing violent video games increases the likelihood for aggressive behavior."

According to the commission, more than 15 meta-analyses have been published examining the links between media violence and aggression. [Craig] Anderson and colleagues, for instance, published a comprehensive meta-analysis of violent video game effects and concluded that the "evidence strongly suggests that exposure to violent video games is a causal risk factor for increased aggressive behavior, aggressive cognition, and aggressive affect and for decreased empathy and prosocial behavior."

In a *Psychiatric Times* interview, psychologist Craig Anderson, PhD, director of the Center for the Study of Violence at Iowa State University, said the evidence for the media violence-aggression link is very strong from every major type of study design: randomized experiments, cross-sectional correlation studies, and longitudinal studies.

In 2007, Anderson's group reported on a longitudinal study of violent video games. The study queried children and their peers as well as teachers on aggressive behaviors and violent media consumption twice during a school year. The researchers found that boys and girls who played a lot of violent video games changed over the school year, becoming more aggressive.

"There now are numerous longitudinal studies by several different research groups around the world, and they all find significant violent video game exposure effects," Anderson said.

In contrast, a longitudinal study published this year by Ferguson and colleagues, which followed 165 boys and girls (aged 10 to 14 years) over 3 years, found no long-term link between violent video games and youth aggression or dating violence.

Studies from Japan, Singapore, Germany, Portugal, and the United States show that "the association between media violence and aggression is similar across cultures," according to Anderson.

"Most recently," he added, "we found that within a high-risk population [incarcerated juvenile offenders], violent video games are associated with violent antisocial behavior, even after controlling for the robust influences of multiple correlates of juvenile delinquency and youth violence, most notably psychopathy."

There is growing evidence, Anderson said, that high exposure to fast-paced violent games can lead to changes in brain function when processing violent images, including dampening of emotional responses to violence and decreases in certain types of executive control. But there also is some evidence that the same type of fast-paced violent games can improve some types of spatial-visual skills, basically, [the] ability to extract visual information from a computer screen.

One of Many Factors

Despite the links between media violence and aggression, Anderson stressed, "media violence is only one of many risk factors for later aggressive and violent behavior. Furthermore, extremely violent behavior never occurs when there is only one risk factor present. Thus, a healthy, well-adjusted person with few risk factors is not going to become a school-shooter just because they start playing a lot of violent video games or watching a lot of violent movies."

One of Anderson's colleagues at Iowa State University, Douglas Gentile, PhD, associate professor of psychology, along with Brad Bushman, PhD, professor of communication and psychology at Ohio State University and professor of communication science at the VU University in Amsterdam, recently published a study that identifies media exposure as 1 of the 6 risk factors for predicting later aggression in 430 children (aged 7 to 11, grades 3 to 5) from Minnesota schools. Besides media violence, the remaining risk factors are bias toward hostility, low parental involvement, participant sex, physical victimization, and prior physical fights.

Knowing students' risk for aggression can help school officials determine which students might be more likely to get in fights or possibly bully other students, according to Gentile, who runs the media research lab at Iowa State University. He said he can get "over 80% accuracy" in predicting which child is at high risk for bullying behavior by knowing 3 things—

"are they a boy, have they gotten in a fight within the past year, and do they consume a lot of media violence."

In discussing their study findings, Gentile and Bushman wrote: "The best single predictor of future aggression in the sample of elementary schoolchildren was past aggression, followed by violent media exposure, followed by having been a victim of aggression."

They added that their risk-factor approach can "cool down" the heated debate on the effects of media violence, since "exposure to violent media is not the only risk factor for aggression or even the most important risk factor, but it is one important risk factor."

"We are interested in using this new approach to measuring the multiple risk factors for aggression in additional samples, and also increasing the number of risk factors we examine (there are over 100 known risk factors for aggression)," Gentile told *Psychiatric Times*. He and colleagues have several other studies under way in several countries.

"I am particularly hopeful that this approach will help the public and professionals realize that media violence is not different from other risk factors for aggression. It's not the largest, nor the smallest," he said. "If there is any important difference at all, it is simply that media violence is easier for parents to control than other risk factors, such as being bullied, having psychiatric illnesses, or living in poverty."

Mass Shootings by the Mentally Disturbed Can Be Mitigated

Dennis Grantham

Dennis Grantham is editor in chief of Behavioral Healthcare.
In the following viewpoint, Grantham reports on a talk by criminal justice psychiatrist Fred Osher on the link between mental illness and violence. Osher says that despite a rash of mass killings by the mentally ill, they are no more likely to commit violent acts than the rest of the population. He further maintains that while it is impossible to predict which individuals with mental problems will act out in a violent manner, there are contributing factors that psychiatrists can identify. Individuals who fit the profile should not be locked up, Osher contends, but secondary screenings by mental health professionals can be useful. Using proper diagnostic techniques can help identify potential criminals and lead to treatment and support that can mitigate the likelihood of violence.

Following a year [2012] in which more mass violence, notably school shootings, focused the attention of lawmakers and the public on the possible linkage between mental illness and criminal violence, longtime community and criminal-justice psychiatrist Fred Osher, who heads the behavioral health division of the Council of State Governments' Justice Center (Bethesda, Md.), asked a capacity crowd at the 2013 National Council Conference [for Behavioral Health] a question: Can we predict or prevent violent behavior?

Mental Illness and Violence

Osher began his discussion by exploring what he called the "complex relationship between mental illness and violence," a relationship that challenges mental health advocates to walk a fine line between two powerful and conflicting perceptions. On one hand, he said, "We must fight against media interpretations that are distorted and stigmatizing toward those who are mentally ill. But we must also own up to the association between some types of mental health and substance use disorders. Denying that such disorders play any role in violent behavior is disingenuous and ultimately counterproductive."

So, he asked, "What can we say about the issue?"

On the positive side, he noted, "We can say that most people with mental illness aren't violent and most violence in our country is not caused by people with mental illness. In fact, people with mental illnesses are far more likely to be the victims of violence, often within their own homes and families." In some cases, he said, this victimization can contribute to future violent behavior.

"Mentally ill people with no history of substance abuse or violence are statistically no more likely than anyone else to behave violently," he added, explaining that demographic factors, such as age, gender, and socioeconomic status "are far better predictors of the likelihood of violence than is the presence or absence of a mental illness."

On the other hand, Osher said, "Mental illness may be a consistent but modest risk factor in the likelihood of violence." While he said there is no clear causal link between mental illness and violence, symptoms associated with some mental illnesses "increase the statistical risk of violence" for some individuals. He explained that those whose mental illnesses result in psychosis, command hallucinations (hearing voices that "command" one to commit harm), paranoia, or paranoid delusions may face—in the absence of effective treatment—a higher risk of future violent behavior.

But there's another even more important risk factor. "We must acknowledge that substance abuse, in people with or without mental illnesses, is a large driver of violent behavior in our communities. And, having said that, it's important that we distinguish violence from criminal behavior." He observed that violent crime is defined by statute as murder, robbery, rape, and assault and that just 3–5 percent of violent crimes are committed by individuals with a mental illness.

It is only in arrests for nonviolent crimes—possession, panhandling and other sometimes petty crimes—that the mentally ill are disproportionately represented. Osher reported that of the 13 million annual arrests in the United States, about one in six, some 2 million, involve individuals with a mental illness. Among men placed under arrest, he said that 15 percent have a mental illness, while the number of mentally ill among women arrested is over 30 percent.

Predicting Violent Behavior—Impossible

Osher introduced the next segment of the discussion with a statement: "We do not have the capability to predict violent actions." Violence of the type witnessed at Sandy Hook Elementary, in Tucson [Arizona], or Virginia Tech represent "extremely rare events." And, he continued, "It is not so easy to predict the occurrence of rare and low probability events." Statistically speaking, "it's a base rate problem—these things just don't happen that often."

Predictive mechanisms are extremely difficult to develop, he added, because each represents "a tradeoff between sensitivity and specificity." For example, he said that any approach that sought to identify all those who might become violent would lead professionals to "overpredict" and "accept a whole lot of false positives." On the other hand, an approach that sought to be highly specific in terms of defining criteria that predict violence would likely mean that "you'll miss a lot of potentially violent individuals down the road." In any event, he debunked the whole notion of prediction.

Rather than risk the high inaccuracy of trying to predict specific instances of individual violence, Osher instead suggested that "professionals can assess the risk for violence" by screening individuals and placing them into what he called "bands of risk." He called on the field to develop greater expertise in using risk assessment tools that combine three factors:

static factors—age, gender, family, criminal history

dynamic (changeable) factors—substance abuse, antisocial thoughts or beliefs, relationships, trust or fear issues

protective (positive) factors—potentially stabilizing or supportive factors including family and family status, employment status, etc.

With these, plus professional judgment, "we can place individuals into bands of risk." Yet he says that screening alone is ineffective unless "you can do something positive about it. The goal is not to screen, assess, and lock someone up." Instead, he says that to be effective, primary prevention steps, such as Mental Health First Aid, that identify at-risk individuals must be accompanied by secondary prevention, which would bring supportive interventions to those whose histories include risk factors for violence.

Triggering an Additional Screen— and Treatment

Osher said that evidence of an individual history of violence, criminal justice contact, or criminal behavior should "trigger" an additional screen in the psychosocial assessment. "We have a chance to get in there, see what happened, and use an intervention to reduce the future possibility of problems." He warned that people who have previous criminal justice involvement "are not inherently more violent" than others, but noted that "they do have more risk factors" and thus merit appropriate interventions to reduce future risk.

Secondary screening and available risk assessment tools are underutilized by behavioral health professionals, whom Osher says don't do a good job of identifying individuals who have histories that include "criminal-genic" factors like past violence or criminal behavior. This screening and follow-up must be appropriately and sensitively used so as not to frighten people away from seeking treatment.

Speaking of the field, he continued that "We're good at the 'bread and butter' responses that involve helping people find employment, improve relationships, find meaningful things to do with their time, and deal with substance abuse, but we're not so good on dealing with antisocial behavior, cognition, fear, and trust issues." Recalling his own training, when personality disorders were said to be "chronic, enduring, and unchangeable," he remarked that "we now have an evolving set of interventions that can help those who have antisocial tendencies and thoughts, that hang with the wrong people. And we've gotta get better, because everyone's goal is to reduce the incidence of violence and criminal behavior in our communities."

"Who Else Is Going to Do This?"

But he noted that the problem goes beyond a failure of professionals to employ the latest screening and interventions. Across the field, he notes a reluctance among some professionals to work with and delve into uncomfortable details with "those people," meaning people with histories of criminal behavior and violence. "Really?" he wondered. "You're working with them anyway," he declared. "And if you don't get into their personal history, you won't know who it was that got out of prison last month." Besides, he continued, "Who else is going to do this? We've got to help them."

"Talking about these things isn't something we're comfortable with—it's not part of our training. Yet, risk assessment and management are professional responsibilities that we have to become better at." The most important thing, he continued, "is to mitigate the risk factors that get people in trouble. Because you know—it's tough to recover if you're in jail."

"The criminal justice system and those we serve within it are part of our community," said Osher, who concluded with three key points:

First, he asserted that "criminal justice and behavioral health are partners in a vision to promote public safety and recovery. Arrest and incarceration," he continued, "are not an acceptable substitute for providing an individual with appropriate care."

Second, he stated that "all behavioral health programs should be 'criminal-justice capable.' The risk of criminal justice should be an expectation, not an exception, something that is part of our planning and service delivery."

Third, he emphasized that while it is impossible at present for anyone to accurately predict an individual incidence of violence, the overall risk of violent criminal behavior can be mitigated by employing tools that identify and assess individuals' risk for future violence and by offering treatment and support.

Dark and Violent Books Help Teens Through Adolescence

Mary Elizabeth Williams

Mary Elizabeth Williams is a staff writer for the online magazine Salon *and the author of* Gimme Shelter: My Three Years Searching for the American Dream.

Williams here responds to an influential piece in the Wall Street Journal, *"Darkness Too Visible," in which critic Meghan Cox Gurdon argues that contemporary young adult (YA) fiction is full of inappropriate material, including brutality, kidnapping, pederasty, and incest. Williams writes that such material has been a staple of YA fiction since she grew up with V.C. Andrews* (Flowers in the Attic) *and Shirley Conran* (Lace) *and that reading such material does not mean that teens will not also seek out more literary authors. Williams further argues that the violence and sexuality in such books are also present in the adolescent world and that reading such books can lead teens to understand that there are sympathetic souls who understand what they are going through. Teens should not be protected from reading about disturbing events, Williams concludes, as the only thing worse than the darkness in fiction and the real world is ignorance.*

Oh jeez, do we really have to have this argument again? All right, fine. Here goes. Contemporary literature has too much sex and violence, and our kids need to be protected from its "depravity." So says critic Meghan Cox Gurdon, in a scorching Saturday editorial about Young Adult [YA] lit [literature] for the *Wall Street Journal* titled "Darkness Too Visible." Let's roll up our sleeves and get to it, shall we?

Mary Elizabeth Williams, "Has Young Adult Fiction Become Too Dark?," Salon, June 6, 2011. This article first appeared in Salon.com, at http://www.Salon.com. An online version remains in the Salon archives. Reprinted with permission.

The Argument Against Dark and Violent YA Literature

In it, Gurdon pulls no punches, railing against an "ever-more-appalling" genre in which "kidnapping and pederasty and incest and brutal beatings are now just part of the run of things in novels directed, broadly speaking, at children from the ages of 12 to 18." She writes, with an unapologetic level of disgust, about the "stomach-clenching detail" in modern YA lit, tracing its "no happy ending" roots back to bleak classics like *Go Ask Alice* [by Anonymous] and Robert Cormier's *I Am the Cheese*, and unfavorably contrasts best-selling author (and darling of the ALA's [American Library Association's] challenged books list) [YA author] Lauren Myracle, and her themes of "homophobia, booze and crystal meth" to the glory era of [American YA author] Judy Blume.

Is there really a problem here, besides, perhaps, the offense to Gurdon's sensibilities? The writer laments that while today's crop of trauma lit "may validate the teen experience," she argues that "it is also possible—indeed, likely—that books focusing on pathologies help normalize them and, in the case of self-harm, may even spread their plausibility and likelihood to young people who might otherwise never have imagined such extreme measures." And she argues that "it is a dereliction of duty not to make distinctions in every other aspect of a young person's life between more and less desirable options."

Gurdon is not exactly some pearls-clutching delicate flower, knee-jerkingly opposed to difficult material. She admits that "reading about homicide doesn't turn a man into a murderer; reading about cheating on exams won't make a kid break the honor code." She lists a few books that she recommends for teens—and they include tough fare like [English author] Mark Haddon's *The Curious Incident of the Dog in the Night-Time* and [American author] Judy Blundell's *What I Saw and How I Lied*. She even admits that the sad reality is

Violent young adult novels such as those in The Hunger Games *trilogy allow teens to tap into their own fears and navigate their way through adolescence.* © Cultura /AP Images.

"many teenagers do not read young adult books at all." Her limitation is in her argument of what constitutes "desirable options."

They're Young Adult, Not Children's Books

As a mother of two voracious readers, one of whom is just shy of the traditional teen lit range, I can certainly vouch that the YA section of your local bookstore can be a pretty damn grim place, rife with everything from angsty vampires to sex abuse to bullying. And no, not all of it is great literature. Remind me again when there was a time when there was nothing but great literature from which to choose? Critics like Gurdon are forever holding the dregs of the present up against the best of the past, which is an unfair and highly loaded argument. You can't compare what's crowding the shelves now with a tiny handful of classics that have endured.

I grew up on Judy Blume too. I also loved [American author] V.C. Andrews. Believe me when I say that the latter's books, with their themes of brutal family abuse and incestuous rape, are trashy as hell—and there was not a girl around for 3,000 miles who could keep her hands off them. And let me further assure you, an entire generation of women managed to devour the *Flowers in the Attic* series without having sex with their brothers. In fact, I can safely say that many of us read [American author Shirley Conran's] *Lace and* [American author J.D.] Salinger *and* [American author James] Baldwin, and the one didn't rot out the others. We read, as teens continue to do now, to be moved, to fall in love with characters, to learn, and to sometimes just explore the things that scared and fascinated us.

But Gurdon doesn't save her scorn for the merely exploitative, bottom of the rack books. She excoriates the "hyperviolent" *Hunger Games* trilogy and [Native American author] Sherman Alexie's acclaimed *The Absolutely True Diary of a Part-Time Indian*, sniffing that "it is no comment on Mr. Alexie's work to say that one depravity does not justify another." And when she clumsily insists, "publishers use the vehicle of fundamental free-expression principles to try to bulldoze coarseness or misery into . . . children's lives," she fails to acknowledge the coarseness and misery already inherent in adolescence. She assumes that coarseness and misery—and profanity, and violence, and sex—are in and of themselves unsuitable subject matter, regardless of the quality of the writing. That's where she goofs up big time.

I take my kids to the library every week, and I've yet to refuse them anything. Frankly, as a parent I've always been a much bigger hardass about their exposure to the Disney princess-to-sassymouthed teen juggernaut than anything involving abuse or a dystopian future. My elder girl has read the dark *Tillerman Cycle* books [by American author Cynthia Voight], and her class this year read [YA author] Lois Lowry's frequently challenged *The Giver*. And when I asked her what she thought of the WSJ [*Wall Street Journal*] piece this weekend, she rolled her tween eyes and said, "Does she get it that they're not called 'children's' books? They're 'young adult.' *Adult.*"

Darkness Is Preferable to Ignorance

That "adult" aspect of reading is scary for many of us. It's our job as parents to protect our kids, even as they slowly move out into the world and further away from our dictates. But there's something almost comical about raising them with tales of big bad wolves and poisoned apples, and then deciding at a certain point that literature is too "dark" for them to handle. Kids are smarter than that. And a kid who is lucky enough to give a damn about the value of reading knows the transformative power of books.

One of the terrific side effects of an obviously click-baiting piece of editorial twaddle like Gurdon's is that it reminds people how many fellow passionate readers there are in the world. That incendiary WSJ piece promptly sparked a tear-jerkingly beautiful Twitter #YAsaves trend full of heartfelt reactions and links to outstandingly reasoned, articulate responses from well-read adults and teens on the value within so much of YA literature and its downright lifesaving effects. As teen blogger Emma eloquently explains, "Good literature rips open all the private parts of us—the parts people like you have deemed too dark, inappropriate, grotesque or abnormal for teens to be feeling—and then they stitch it all back together again before we even realize they're not talking about us." That's why it matters; why, in the name of protecting teens, we can't shut them off from the outlet of experiencing difficult events and feelings in the relative safety and profound comfort of literature. Darkness isn't the enemy. But ignorance always is.

For Further Discussion

1. How did Collins's early experiences as the child of a career military man influence her later writings? Refer to viewpoints by Claire Armistead, Rick Margolis, and Hillel Italie to inform your answer.

2. According to Collins, what message does she want young people to take away from her books concerning the nature of warfare? Consider viewpoints by Claire Armistead, Rick Margolis, and Hillel Italie to formulate your answer.

3. According to Brian Bethune, what elements of *The Hunger Games* trilogy have led to the books' popularity?

4. Is the war against the Capitol justified? Is war ever justified? Do the atrocities of the Capitol inevitably lead the districts to rebel, and is the rebellion worth it in the end? Refer to viewpoints by Louis Melançon and Marty Troyer to inform your answer.

5. Is the first Hunger Games (and the later Quarter Quell) a realistic depiction of violent battle, or as Paul K. Chappell asserts, are Collins's battle scenes simplistic and inaccurate?

6. Does media violence influence violence in society, and are books such as *The Hunger Games* and its successors too violent? Consider viewpoints by Robert M. Schwartz, James Hirsen, and Arline Kaplan to formulate your answer.

For Further Reading

M.T. Anderson, *Feed*. Cambridge, MA: Candlewick Press, 2002.

Margaret Atwood, *MaddAddam*. New York: Nan A. Talese/ Doubleday, 2013.

———, *Oryx and Crake*. New York: Anchor Books, 2004.

———, *The Year of the Flood*. New York: Anchor Books, 2010.

Anthony Burgess, *A Clockwork Orange*. New York: W.W. Norton, 1962.

Orson Scott Card, *Ender's Game*. New York: T. Doherty Associates, 1985.

Suzanne Collins, *Gregor and the Code of Claw*. New York: Scholastic, 2007.

———, *Gregor and the Curse of the Warmbloods*. New York: Scholastic, 2005.

———, *Gregor and the Marks of Secret*. New York: Scholastic, 2006.

———, *Gregor and the Prophecy of Bane*. New York: Scholastic, 2004.

———, *Gregor the Overlander*. New York: Scholastic, 2003.

James Dashner, *The Maze Runner*. New York: Delacorte Press, 2009.

William Golding, *Lord of the Flies*. London: Faber & Faber, 1954.

Aldous Huxley, *Brave New World*. Garden City, NY: Doubleday, Doran & Company, 1932.

Stephen King, *The Running Man*. New York: Signet, 1982.

Lois Lowry, *The Giver*. Boston, MA: Houghton Mifflin, 1993.

George Orwell, *Nineteen Eighty-Four*. London: Secker and Warburg, 1949.

Ayn Rand, *Anthem*. London: Cassell, 1938.

Veronica Roth, *Allegiant*. New York: Katherine Tegen Books, 2013.

———, *Divergent*. New York: Katherine Tegen Books, 2011.

———, *Insurgent*. New York: Katherine Tegen Books, 2012.

Koushun Takami, *Battle Royale*. San Francisco, CA: VIZ Media, 2003.

Bibliography

Books

Balaka Basu, Katherine R. Broad, and Carrie Hintz, eds. — *Contemporary Dystopian Fiction for Young Adults: Brave New Teenagers.* New York: Routledge, 2013.

Noah Berlatsky, ed. — *Media Violence.* Detroit, MI: Greenhaven Press, 2012.

Denise M. Bonilla, ed. — *School Violence.* New York: H.W. Wilson Co., 2000.

M. Keith Booker, ed. — *Contemporary Speculative Fiction.* Ipswich, MA: Salem Press 2013.

M. Keith Booker, ed. — *The Dystopian Impulse in Modern Literature: Fiction as Social Criticism.* Westport, CT: Greenwood Press, 1994.

Valerie Estelle Frankel — *Katniss the Cattail: An Unauthorized Guide to Names and Symbols in Suzanne Collins' The Hunger Games.* United States: LitCrit Press, 2012.

Louise I. Gerdes, Ed. — *Violence.* Detroit, MI: Greenhaven Press, 2008.

Elie Godsi — *Violence and Society: Making Sense of Madness and Badness.* Ross-on-Wye, UK: PCCS Books, 2014.

David M. Haugen and Susan Musser, eds.   *Media Violence.* Detroit, MI: Greenhaven Press, 2009.

Tom Henthorne   *Approaching the Hunger Games Trilogy: A Literary and Cultural Analysis.* Jefferson, NC: McFarland & Co. Publishers, 2012.

Carrie Hintz and Elaine Ostry, eds.   *Utopian and Dystopian Writing for Children and Young Adults.* New York: Routledge, 2003.

Sheila Llanas   *How to Analyze the Works of Suzanne Collins.* Minneapolis, MN: ABDO Pub. Co, 2013.

Sara Petersson   *The Hunger Games by Suzanne Collins: Entertainment or Social Criticism?* Lund, Sweden: Lund University, 2012.

Mary F. Pharr and Leisa A. Clark, eds.   *Of Bread, Blood, and the Hunger Games: Critical Essays on the Suzanne Collins Trilogy.* Jefferson, NC: McFarland & Co., 2012.

Doreen Piano, ed.   *Violence.* Detroit, MI: Greenhaven Press, 2007.

Steven Pinker   *The Better Angels of Our Nature: Why Violence Has Declined.* New York: Viking, 2011.

Cath Senker   *Violence.* Mankato, MN: Smart Apple Media, 2010.

Neil L. Whitehead, ed.   *Violence.* Santa Fe, NM: School of American Research, 2004.

Periodicals and Internet Sources

Paul M. Barrett   "Does Violent Media Lead to Violent Behavior? No, Says Paul Barrett," *Variety*, January 18, 2013.

Brian Bethune   "'The Hunger Games': Your Kids Are Angrier than You Think," *Maclean's*, April 2, 2012.

Susan Dominus   "Suzanne Collins's War Stories for Kids," *New York Times*, April 8, 2011.

Jonathan Foreman   "London Aflame: What Happens When You Let Teenagers Run Your Country," *National Review*, August 29, 2011.

Linda A. Gann and Karen Gavigan   "The Other Side of Dark: Is It Really the End of the World? Examining the Nature of Young Adult Dystopian Literature," *Voice of Youth Advocates*, August 2012.

Meghan Cox Gurdon   "Darkness Too Visible," *Wall Street Journal*, June 4, 2011.

A. Waller Hastings   "*The Hunger Games*: Dystopia and the Adolescent Mind," Academia.edu, October 15, 2010. http://www.academia .edu/2144619/The_Hunger_Games _Dystopia_and_the_Adolescent_Mind.

Duncan Hewitt   "Chinese Authorities Crack Down on Reality Television," *Newsweek International*, April 2, 2012.

IndianTelevision
.com

"NCPCR Issues Guidelines for TV Shows," November 29, 2011. http://www.indiantelevision.com /headlines/y2k11/nov/nov267.php.

Ted Johnson

"Shootings Spur Media Scrutiny: Pols, Pundits Revive Old Debate," *Daily Variety*, July 23, 2012.

Melissa Klein

"Gang Grief: Violence Wounds Teens and Communities," *Current Health 2*, March 2009.

Carol Lloyd

"Help! My Child Has Been Reaped," Great Schools. http://www.greatschools .org/students/media-kids/633 -hunger-games-too-violent.gs.

Andre Mayer

"*Hunger Games* Can't Match the Cruelty of *Lord of the Flies*," CBC News, March 22, 2012.

Lyn
Miller-Lachmann

"War, Peace and The Hunger Games," *Albany Times Union*, September 27, 2010.

Nerdy Girl Notes

"A True American Horror Story: Violence, Childhood, and The Hunger Games," http://nerdygirlnotes .com/2012/04/20/a-true-american -horror-story-violence-childhood -and-the-hunger-games/.

Randy Pitchford and Dave Grossman — "Point . . . Counterpoint: Do Videogames Inspire Violent Behavior? Absolutely Not, Says Vidgame Developer Randy Pitchford. Absolutely Yes, Says Lt. Col. David Grossman," *Variety*, Winter 2013.

Travis Prinzi — "The Hunger Games: Panem's Politics," The Hog's Head, February 16, 2010. http://thehogshead.org/the-hunger-games-panems-politics-4426/.

Emily Sohn — "Hunger Games: Confronting Violence in Tween Books," Discovery.com, April 3, 2012. http://news.discovery.com/human/hunger-games-parents-120403.htm.

James Stern and Mike Hammond — "Point . . . Counterpoint: Are 300 Million Guns in America Too Many? Yes, Says Film Exec James Stern. No, Says Gun Owners of America's Mike Hammond," *Variety*, Winter 2013.

Andrew Stuttaford — "Quidditch, It's Not," *National Review Online*, July 30, 2012.

Index

CPSIA information can be obtained
at www.ICGtesting.com
Printed in the USA
FFOW04n0734191214
9704FF